PENGUIN BOOKS

THE PENGUIN FINANCIAL G[...]
TO A SUCCESSFUL RETIREMEN[...]

Alison Mitchell is presenter of *Money Box*, the Radio 4 family finance programme, and the financial adviser on *The Jimmy Young Programme* on Radio 2. She appears on BBC1's *Bazaar* and Channel 4 *News* and writes a regular column for the *Reader's Digest*. In addition to being family finance expert on BBC *Breakfast Time* for six years she was, before that, with the *Sunday Express* and *The Times*. Her most recent books are *The New Penguin Guide to Personal Finance* and *Your Money – Straight and Simple*.

Wendy Elkington is Deputy Editor of 'Money Mail', the *Daily Mail*'s personal finance section, and writes regularly for several magazines, including *Ideal Home*, *Money Observer* and *Expat Investor*. In 1990 she won the Pensions and Investment Journalist of the Year award, and has been short-listed for the Personal Finance Journalist of the Year, Insurance Writer of the Year and Medical Insurance Writer of the Year awards. Among her other books are *How to Beat Your Bank Manager* and *The Women's Institute Guide to Insurance*.

Alison Mitchell and Wendy Elkington

THE PENGUIN FINANCIAL GUIDE TO A SUCCESSFUL RETIREMENT

PENGUIN BOOKS
IN ASSOCIATION WITH TOWRY LAW GROUP

PENGUIN BOOKS

Published by the Penguin Group
Penguin Books Ltd, 27 Wrights Lane, London W8 5TZ, England
Penguin Books USA Inc., 375 Hudson Street, New York, New York 10014, USA
Penguin Books Australia Ltd, Ringwood, Victoria, Australia
Penguin Books Canada Ltd, 10 Alcorn Avenue, Toronto, Ontario, Canada M4V 3B2
Penguin Books (NZ) Ltd, 182–190 Wairau Road, Auckland 10, New Zealand

Penguin Books Ltd, Registered Offices: Harmondsworth, Middlesex, England

First published 1993
10 9 8 7 6 5 4 3 2 1

Typeset by Datix International Limited, Bungay, Suffolk
Printed in England by Clays Ltd, St Ives plc

Contents

Contents

Acknowledgements

Checking the facts of a personal finance book such as this is always a Herculean task. Our grateful thanks to all who helped in the laborious process.

Towry Law Group, the nationwide firm of independent financial advisers, have been particularly involved. Our thanks to marketing director Clive Scott-Hopkins and to John Bridel, Paul Rylatt and Peter Stimpson.

Thanks also to Jackie Manning at National Savings and Paddy Ross and Joan Lord at the Leith Money Advice Centre. And to Roger Gilbert for his considerable help.

Alison Mitchell and Wendy Elkington
London, 1993

1 When I'm Sixty-four

Life would be a lot simpler if we knew when we were going to die. We could plan our finances so that there would be no surprises to ambush our savings along the way. We could live life in the pink, secure in the knowledge our finances would be in the black.

But, of course, life is not like that – and maybe that is for the best. The Scottish philanthropist Andrew Carnegie claimed that a man who died rich, died disgraced. And to prove the point he gave away most of his vast fortune. For most of us, however, dying rich is vastly preferable to living poor.

During our routine working lives, we tread the grapes. Retirement ought to signal the start of the vintage years for corks to be popped and champagne savoured. For far from being the end of an era, retirement can be a powerful springboard to catapult us into the golden years – provided we have some gold to go with them.

That is what this book is all about. And by reading this far, you have taken the first crucial step in planning for a successful retirement.

In Britain, we're obsessed with our age. And when it comes to form filling, age seems to be the most sought-after personal detail after name. But, of course, there is nothing magical about a man's sixty-fifth or a woman's sixtieth birthday. Candles on the cake give no clue about the strength of the flames which burn within.

Compulsory retirement at sixty-five and sixty was introduced largely for political and economic reasons and has little to do with physical and mental well-being. Many sixty-somethings are still in their prime – indeed some are just getting started. Lord King, although in his mid-seventies, was still flying high as chairman of British Airways. Bernard Shaw was in his eighties when he penned *Pygmalion*. Titian painted his best pictures when he was nearly ninety. Churchill and Reagan ran countries, thousands more octogenarians run marathons.

But now that retirement allows you to dance to the more gentle tune of a carriage clock on the mantelpiece rather than an alarm clock on the bedside table, what should you do?

Anything you like. For perhaps the first time in your life you'll be free to do exactly as you choose – no family to think about, no boss to please, no set thing to do.

And a pleasant surprise might be to discover just how well off you are – freed from mortgage or school fees. Yet in our grandparents' day, stopping work often meant the start of the end – scrimping through an uncomfortable old age into an early death. State and company pensions have changed all that. Provided you have the right, positive mental attitude, a well-organized financial plan – that you'll be taken through in easy-to-follow steps in this book – will ensure you don't put a foot wrong for a happy retirement.

All right, maybe money can't buy happiness, but it will help you rent it for a lifetime.

Life expectancy			
	Age on retirement		
	55	60	65
Men	78	79	80
Women	83	83	84

As we indicated at the start, the difficulty is that we don't know how long we'll live. What is called for is a successful juggling act – spend enough to enjoy your retirement, yet save enough for the later years. The average person who lives to retirement soars easily past the three score years and ten that one feels entitled to. So it is worth remembering two factors that should affect your spending:

- increasing costs
- inflation.

Increasing costs. As you get older your expenses will rise. As you get less fit, less able, stiffness, aching bones and lack of mobility will mean that you'll have to start paying for things you've always done yourself like gardening, cleaning the windows, even shopping. So the older you get the more expensive your life becomes. Ultimately you may even have to pay for some form of nursing or residential care, which will make huge inroads into any savings you have.

Inflation. If you're old enough to remember the double-figure inflation rates in the 1970s you'll know what that does to the spending power of pensions and the capital value of savings. You may look ahead now to a pension that seems more than adequate – after all, twenty years ago a pension of £8,000 a year would have seemed like a king's ransom, but it wouldn't keep you in clover now. Inflation of 5 per cent halves the value of your money in fifteen years.

So to check out whether or not you could actually live on your pension, here's a tip. Use today's money and today's values. If your pension promises you two thirds of final salary, work out if you could live on two thirds of your current pay cheque every month for the rest of your life. And if you couldn't, then try to do something now to increase the value of the pay-out that you are going to get.

To help you work out the cost of your retirement, there's a Budget Planner at the end of this chapter. Spend a wet Sunday filling it in as accurately as you can. Of course it can give you no more than a rough guide to your likely spending – and don't underestimate what your hobbies and holidays will cost you.

Remember too that you'll spend a lot more on heating and

cooking simply because you are at home during the day – though a lot less on commuting, office clothes, business lunches and colleagues' wedding presents.

And you'll be able to use your time to save money, where in the past you used money to save time. You can cut the cost of travel by going off-peak, get cheap theatre and cinema tickets on less popular days, get cheap haircuts at the beginning of the week and avoid expensive times in restaurants.

Why read this book?

This book has been written to help you with your retirement. If you're reading it before you give up work, you'll be able to plan ahead financially to make the best use of the years before retirement. But if you are already on a pension, this book will show you how to get the best deal out of your investments, your pensions, your insurance, your savings. It will take you from the easy savings choices right through to the ins and outs of inheritance tax planning and passing on your money before you go to the great golf-course in the sky. Whatever your financial dexterity, this book will improve it. For some readers it will teach them all they need to know about planning a successful retirement. For others it will give them the confidence to ask the right questions of their financial adviser. Whichever group you are in, you'll save a lot more than you spent on this book.

COUNTDOWN TO RETIREMENT

Twentysomething

Once you get a proper job, ask about the company pension. Join it, or take out a personal pension plan. Don't over-commit yourself at this stage because you can't get the cash out again until you retire. But money invested in a pension fund at this stage grows like Topsy.

Thirtysomething

You should certainly be in a pension scheme by now. Join your employers' scheme or set up a personal pension scheme.

Fortysomething

Make sure you are not underfunding your pension. Keep an eye on any bits of pension you have left behind on job changing and move them elsewhere if they could do better.

Fiftysomething

Do some careful checking to make sure you can afford to retire on your pension. If you can't, make the necessary moves, including your full ration of PEPs and TESSAs. Think about where you'll live in retirement, what you'll do about the mortgage, when you want to retire. Check with the DSS that your National Insurance record is up to date. If it is not, try to make up as much as you can.

Just before you retire, write to any company schemes you are in to alert them to your forthcoming retirement so that they can get the pay-outs ready.

Sixtysomething

Women can retire on a state pension at sixty if they qualify through their own National Insurance contributions; otherwise they will have to wait until their husband qualifies for his at sixty-five. If you postpone it, you get more when it does pay out but it stops rising in value after you have postponed for five years. Check with the Inland Revenue so that you get the age allowance once you reach sixty-five.

Budget planner

SPENDING

Fixed	*Occasional*
Mortgage/rent	Car bills
Council tax	Holidays
Water rates	Eating out
House insurance	Hobbies
Gas/electricity/coal	Christmas and birthdays
Phone/fax	Sport
TV/video rental, licence	Replacement items
Car insurance	Garden
Road tax	Hairdresser
	Theatre/cinema

Everyday

Supermarket/shops

Petrol/bus fares

Papers and milk

Books and magazines

Subtotal	*Subtotal*

Total spending

INCOME

Pensions

DSS benefits

Interest and dividends

Other income

Total income

BALANCE

Total income

Total spending

Surplus/deficit

PART ONE

BEFORE RETIREMENT

2 Investing for Your Retirement

Capital growth or income · tax and your investments · savings accounts · TESSAs · PEPs · friendly societies · unit and investment trusts · shares · with-profit bonds · alternative investments

See also: Chapter 11, Investing at Retirement; Chapter 17, Investing after Retirement

Turning fifty can be a financial watershed leading into the decade when you start to feel well off. Gone, hopefully, are the days when you struggled to pay the mortgage, juggle with the school fees and claw your way up the salary scale. With luck the children will be off your hands, a wife may have gone back to work, the mortgage should be manageable on what may be a good salary. Your expenses too will have soared: you probably enjoy better holidays, more meals out and an older claret than you did in your twenties. None the less this is the time to start putting a nest-egg aside for your retirement.

CAPITAL GROWTH OR INCOME?

Before you can decide where to invest your extra money you have to know what you want from it, and the first decision is whether you want capital growth or income from your money.

Capital growth. Investing for capital growth means you want to preserve the value of your money in the years to come. If

£9,000 will buy you a car now, then you need that sum to be able to buy you a similar sort of car in say five or ten years' time. An investment for capital growth should hold its value against the ravages of inflation, so that if the price of the car has risen to £12,000, with luck your lump sum will have kept pace. In order to do this, you have to take a risk with your money. Most investments for capital growth are in some way linked to shares, which, as we all know by now, go down as well as up. The more risk you take, the higher are the chances of capital growth, and the higher the chances of losing all or part of your investment.

Tax

There are few investment decisions made in life that don't require a look at the tax situation first.

Where you put your money often depends on whether you are a non-taxpayer, a basic-rate taxpayer or a high-rate payer – and investing for growth is no different.

Take savings certificates, for example. These are a five-year hold because the interest is paid on a sliding scale with the highest rate coming in the final year, and the interest is paid tax-free. Savings certificates are therefore ideal for a high-rate taxpayer. After all, if you are losing 40 per cent in tax off any interest you receive from a savings account, then a tax-free investment gives you the equivalent of 40 per cent more. A savings certificate paying an average of 5.75 per cent a year tax-free over five years is equivalent to getting 9.6 per cent from a building-society account for a person paying tax at 40 per cent, and 7.6 per cent to a 25 per cent taxpayer. At a time when savings certificates offer less than 6 per cent, you'd be unlikely to find a risk-free investment paying 9.6 per cent or even 7.6 per cent.

Non-taxpayers of course could do much better in an ordinary savings account, provided they remember to sign the appropriate form so that they don't get the tax deducted. So before you invest, check the tax situation.

> **Tip**
> If you are a high-rate taxpayer and your spouse pays at the basic rate – or you pay tax and your spouse doesn't – make sure your savings are in the name of the person paying the lower rate. That way less tax will be deducted from the interest and you'll both be the richer for it.

GOING FOR INCOME

Income. If you need interest from your money to supplement your salary or pension, then you are investing for income. In general, you should put your capital in a high-interest ultra-safe building society, bank or National Savings account and get the best rate of interest you can. There's no risk, but there's not much reward either. And, for most people, this is not the time for taking income from their savings.

GOING FOR GROWTH – THE OPTIONS

Savings account

What it is. A bank or building-society account that provides a safe, accessible home for your emergency cash. Everyone, no matter how rich, should start here. You should also have a buffer account with the money tied up for longer, perhaps three months, maybe even a year, just in case you need a sizeable sum at a time when your stock-market-linked investments are looking jaded.

Tax. Bank and building society accounts deduct tax at basic rate – currently 25 per cent. If you know you are going to be a non-taxpayer you can sign form R85 at your branch and the interest will be added gross (that is without tax being deducted). If you pay tax at 20 per cent you can claim back the difference, but if you pay at 40 per cent you will have to declare the interest on your tax form and pay up.

Pros. Easy to get at, a completely safe home for your first tranche of money.

Cons. No capital growth here, only interest.

TESSAs

What it is. Tax Exempt Special Savings Accounts are run by most banks and building societies. This is really a five-year account and to qualify you have to follow the rules:

- you can only have one account
- you must be over eighteen
- the maximum you can invest over the five years is £9,000 – up to £3,000 in the first year, up to £1,800 in the next three years and up to £600 in the final year.

Tax. The interest on the account is completely tax-free if you leave it in for the five years. If you withdraw the interest during the term then a notional tax is deducted, but at the end of the five-year term you get it back. However, if you withdraw more than the interest, the account is closed.

Pros. Ideal for ordinary and high-rate taxpayers who don't mind tying their money up for five years, but not such a good idea for non-taxpayers, as they might get higher rates elsewhere.

Cons. Read the small print of the accounts before you sign up. Some have high charges, others will penalize you if you switch to a different bank or building society and some insist that you keep a lump sum in a 'feeder' account. As a rule of thumb, those offering the highest rates of interest also have the most penalty clauses.

PEP

What it is. Personal Equity Plans are a form of stock exchange investment with good tax advantages. You can put up to £6,000 a year into a PEP (£12,000 for married couples) and a further £3,000 each into what is known as a single-company PEP.

PEPs are run by professional fund managers. Some of your money will be invested in British or European shares either directly or through a unit or investment trust, or some of it may be left as cash. The single-company PEP, as the name suggests, is an investment in one company, for up to £3,000 a year. There is no time-limit on this type of investment, you can leave your money in for as long or as short a period as you like, though, as with most share-related investments, it really needs to run for two or three years to show much chance of growth.

Tax. The great joy of a PEP is that the income and capital gain is completely tax-free.

Pros. The main advantage of a PEP is the tax treatment. If you are an income-tax or capital-gains-tax payer you'll do better taxwise in a unit-trust or investment-trust PEP than if you go straight into the trust itself. Ideal for high-rate payers.

Cons. Some PEPs have high charges, which could wipe out the tax advantages, and if you don't pay capital gains tax there may be no good reason to invest in something that avoids it.

PIBS

What it is. Permanent Interest Bearing Shares are one of the newest additions to the investment market. They are building society shares which are listed on the London Stock Exchange and can be bought and sold just like shares.

Tax. Income tax at 25 per cent is deducted from interest, but can be claimed back. No capital gains tax is paid on profits.

Pros. The interest rate is fixed at the outset and is payable at six-monthly intervals.

Cons. In the unlikely event of a building society being wound up, PIBS investors would be last in line as creditors and investors are not covered by the building society compensation scheme. To sell your shares, your broker must be able to find a willing buyer – not always easy.

Friendly society

What it is. You can invest up to £18 a month, £200 a year or a lump sum of £800 in a ten-year savings plan with a friendly society. The money will then be reinvested by them either in an ultra-safe building society account or in, say, unit trusts which could give you capital growth or in a with-profit fund.

Tax. The scheme is completely tax-free, so if the money is linked to a building society, taxpayers will get a better rate than the advertised savings-account rate.

Pros. Ideal for basic and top-rate taxpayers because no tax is paid on any gains.

Cons. The investment is limited by government regulations capping the maximum you can pay in. Not a good investment for non-taxpayers. And the charges are relatively high, especially in the first year.

Unit trust

What it is. A unit trust is a pool of investors' money that is usually used to buy a range of shares. It allows the investor to cash in on a professional fund manager's expertise, at a cost, and to spread the risk by buying a small share in lots of investments. Unit trusts can be general funds, or specialist ones investing in small companies, green shares, Europe, the Far East, America or whatever – the range is very wide indeed. Most investors start with a lump sum of £500 or more, but you can invest on a regular monthly or annual basis. Unit trusts are bought directly from unit trust companies, through a stockbroker or financial intermediary, or by cutting coupons from a financial newspaper or magazine.

Tax. Unit trusts are taxed like other investments. You pay income tax at your highest rate on any dividends that you receive and capital gains tax on any profits you make if you breach the CGT barrier in any tax year.

Pros. Allows you to invest in the stock market while reducing your risk by spreading your investment over more shares.

Cons. Charges can be high. Annual management charges can run to 1.5 per cent of your investment and the 'spread' (that's the difference between the price you buy units at and the price you sell them at on any given day) can amount to 7 per cent of the unit price.

Investment trust

What it is. An investment trust works in a similar way to a unit trust in that it pools investors' money, often borrows a bit more and invests the lot in shares. The difference is that once an investment trust is up and running it cannot take in any new money, so the only way to buy into an investment trust is through its shares. You can either deal through a stockbroker or directly with the investment trust company if it has a regular savings plan: there will of course be a commission charged for the purchase – and the subsequent sale. Like unit trusts you can buy general or specialist investment trusts and the more specialist the trust the higher the risk and the higher the chances of showing a loss or making a killing.

Tax. Investment trusts are treated in the same way as shares – you pay income tax on dividends and CGT, if you qualify, on any profits that you make.

Pros. A good way to spread your risk; in comparison with unit trusts, investment trusts tend to perform better in the long term. There is the added bonus that the investment trust might be taken over by another company at a higher share price and you usually buy at a discount to the net asset value.

Cons. This is an investment for the slightly more financially sophisticated; your investment will slip if the market in general falls, or your fund-management group underperforms.

Shares

What it is. When you buy shares in a British company you are buying a very small stake in that company, and so become a part-owner. You'll get a share in the profits – the dividend – and the share price will rise and fall in line with how well or badly the company is performing. Ultimately, if it goes bust, you'll lose the cash you invested. You buy shares through a stockbroker and commissions vary, though most charge upwards of £20 for small deals, 1.65 per cent for larger ones. (The same for selling.)

Tax. You pay income tax on any dividends you receive. Tax will already have been deducted before you receive them; if you are a high-rate payer you will have to pay 20 per cent more; a non-taxpayer can claim tax back. Capital gains tax will be levied on any profits you make over the CGT level in any one tax year – £5,800 in 1993–4.

Pros. You can make a great deal of money out of shares when prices rise or if you spot a winner. If you invest in a flagship company like ICI or Glaxo you should do quite well over the medium to longer term, and if you hit a company that is on a roll you can do very well indeed, much better than in a lot of other investments.

Cons. You can of course lose a lot investing in shares. If your company is hit by the recession, has bad management or is overtaken by technology the share price will languish and the dividend may be cut. That is the risk you take with your investment. You also need quite a lot of money to start with. Unless you can afford to risk £3,000 or more, and won't be suicidal if you lose it all, don't play this game. But if you do, stick to blue chips if you want to play safe.

With-profit bonds

What it is. Sometimes known as single-premium life bonds, these offer above-average returns and low risk. You are, in fact, investing in the with-profits funds of life-insurance companies. You can invest a lump sum instead of paying regular premiums, and your money, along with everyone else's in the fund, is invested in shares, fixed-interest securities, cash deposits and property. Every year an annual bonus is added to your policy, which cannot be removed. In good years, some of the profits from the fund will be held back in reserve, to be used in leaner times.

Tax. Basic-rate tax is deemed to be paid by the insurance company, and non-taxpayers cannot claim it back. Ordinary-rate taxpayers pay no more tax; higher-rate taxpayers can take income of up to 5 per cent a year of the original investment free of personal tax every year, but if they take more, then they will be charged the difference. You also pay the difference when you cash in the bonds, but you may not be a high-rate taxpayer then.

Pros. These bonds offer capital gain rather than income and if you are a high-rate taxpayer now, but won't be when you retire, they are ideal for putting off the day when you pay the tax to a time when you will be paying at a lower rate.

Cons. Insurance companies discourage short-term investment by making a charge of up to 3 per cent for anyone wanting out in the first few years. There is a spread of 5 per cent on the buying and selling prices of the bonds but that can be reduced if you are putting in a sizeable sum.

Other alternatives

There are plenty of other ways of investing for growth, though most carry a higher element of risk. The riskier they are, the greater is the potential for making a killing. How much risk you want to take depends on how much money you have and how much you are prepared to lose. If you can't afford to lose it, you shouldn't be playing the game.

BES schemes

The government is phasing these out from the end of December 1993, so move quickly if you want to take advantage. And stick to property schemes with a firm date when you can get your money out. The great advantage is that you can claim back the tax on your investment. High-rate taxpayers putting £10,000 into a BES scheme write a cheque for £10,000, and at the end of the year get £4,000 back from the Inland Revenue. So they only risk £6,000 because they'd have lost the rest to the taxman anyway. If you want to go ahead and put money into a BES scheme before the time runs out, take advice first.

Alternative investments

This usually means investing in your hobby – be it fine wine, antiques, stamps, coins, paintings, gold or first editions. You'll only make money if you really know what you are doing – in which case you already know more about it than we do.

3 Pensions for the Employee

Everything you need to know about company pension schemes and personal contributions

See also: Chapter 4, Personal Pensions; Chapter 5, State Pensions and SERPs; Chapter 6, Pensions and Job Changers; Chapter 12, Pensions and the Cash Sum

The Maxwell scandal has made people think very carefully about the security of their company pension. But whether you already belong to the firm's scheme or are thinking of joining, the point to keep in mind is that the overwhelming majority of funds are well managed by honest people and they have plenty of cash in the kitty to pay you a pension when you retire.

Why you should join

Nearly 12 million employees, half the workforce, belong to a company pension scheme. Britain has one of the best developed private pension systems in the European Community and there are several important reasons why most people should join the company scheme if there is one:

- The state pensions will not pay you enough to ensure you have a comfortable retirement (see Chapter 5).
- You get tax relief at your top tax rate – so for every £100 paid in, the net cost is only £75 for basic-rate taxpayers and £60 for higher-rate taxpayers.
- The fund grows free of all taxes.

Before Retirement

- You can draw a tax-free lump sum when you retire.
- Your own contributions – typically 5 per cent of pay – are often small compared to the amount paid in by your employer. Some schemes are non-contributory, with the company paying the entire cost.
- Your family will be protected if you die before retirement.

Who can join?

Since 1988, membership of a pension fund has been voluntary and does not have to be a condition of employment. If you are already a member, you can leave if you want to, but you may not be allowed back in again. The rules of the fund will decide who is eligible, but the following rules often apply:

- Conditions have to be the same for both men and women.
- Often a minimum age – perhaps twenty – or a minimum length of service – such as one year – is specified.
- Part-time workers are often excluded.
- You generally cannot join if you are within five years of retirement.

Different types of schemes

There are two main types of scheme.

Final-salary

This is the most common and pays you a pension linked to the amount you are earning when you retire. Good schemes work on what is known as a one-sixtieth basis and your pension will be calculated as 1/60 of your final salary for every year you have worked. What this means is that if you work for the same employer for thirty years you will get 30/60, i.e. half, your final salary as a pension. Poor schemes may only pay 1/80 for each year. If your pension is linked to your final salary the advantage is that it is protected against inflation.

Money-purchase

Your pension will not be 'defined' at the outset and there is no automatic link to final salary. Cash is invested to provide a fund on retirement, which is then used to buy an annuity (see Chapter 12). How much pension you get depends on:

- how much you and your employer put in
- how well the fund grows over the years
- how much pension your fund can buy when you retire.

These schemes are becoming more popular, as employees have in effect their own individual pension account. If you change jobs, it is easy to identify how much cash has accumulated and take it with you to your next employment.

No obligation

You no longer have to join your company scheme, although most people should. The law now says that employees can have their own personal pension plan instead, but the drawback is the employer is not obliged to contribute to it. Personal pensions are much more important to employees whose company does not have an in-house scheme (see Chapter 4).

Contracting out

If you belong to your company's pension scheme you are likely to be contracted out of the government SERPs – this stands for State Earnings Related Pension scheme. The final-salary company scheme has to guarantee a pension as good as SERPs (known as a guaranteed minimum pension – GMP); in practice they should do a lot better. In return, both employer and employee pay reduced National Insurance contributions. At retirement the GMP has to be increased annually in line with inflation.

PENSION LIMITATIONS

Your pension will be affected by a number of factors.

Years with employer. Final-salary schemes pay on the basis of a fraction – say one sixtieth – for every year of fund membership.

Final salary. If you are lucky, your pension will be worked out on your salary prior to retirement. However, the actual final-salary figure is more likely to be an average of the best consecutive three years out of the last ten or some similar calculation.

Integration. About half of all company schemes reduce the pension by 'integrating' it with the state scheme. This means that total earnings will be reduced for pension purposes by an allowance for the basic state pension. This has the effect of reducing your final pensionable salary.

Inland Revenue rules. The taxman has a set of rules which could limit the amount of your pension:

- The maximum you can get is limited to two thirds of final salary.
- Maximum earnings on which contributions and pension are based is limited to £75,000. This cap applies only to schemes set up after the 1989 Budget or to members who joined a scheme after 1 June 1989.
- The maximum contribution which an employee is allowed to make is limited to 15 per cent of earnings, subject to the limit described above.

Tax-free lump sum. Some public-sector schemes automatically provide a cash lump sum as well as a pension on retirement. With most private schemes you can choose to give up part of your pension in return for a tax-free cash payment – called commutation. This will naturally mean a lower pension, but most people do take the maximum allowed – up to one and a half times final salary. The tax-free lump sum may also be subject to the 'cap' described above. Women who joined the scheme prior to the 1989 deadline can expect to give up £1 a year of pension for every £11 in cash, while a man aged sixty-five can expect to give up around £1 of pension for every £9 of lump sum. After 1989 a unisex rate of £1 of pension for every £12 of lump sum applies. Taking the maximum lump sum is generally a good idea because:

- It is tax-free, whereas pension income will be taxed.
- If you still need extra income, you can invest the money or buy an annuity which has favourable tax treatment (see Chapter 12).
- If your health is poor, take the maximum allowable when you retire. Remember – at least part of your pension dies with you.
- If your health is very poor, you may be able to commute your whole pension for a lump sum with Inland Revenue approval.

DEATH-IN-SERVICE BENEFITS

Company pension schemes provide valuable cover for the family should you die before you reach retirement age. These include:

- a tax-free lump sum to your spouse or partner based on a multiple of your current pensionable earnings; good schemes pay out four times salary although many funds pay out less than this
- a spouse's pension, which is normally based on the employee's current salary in relation to the number of years of existing fund membership plus the number of years to normal retirement age
- a refund of pension contributions, possibly with interest
- an allowance to children under eighteen or in full-time education, if the scheme is a good one.

PENSIONS EQUALITY

Company pension schemes often used to specify that women could retire at sixty and draw a pension, while men had to wait until their sixty-fifth birthday. However, as a result of recent changes in the law, employers cannot make women retire earlier than men, and many schemes are changing the rules so that both men and women retire at the same age – typically at the age of sixty-five, though some have opted for sixty or sixty-three.

Most have chosen to raise the pension age for women, rather than reducing it for men, as the latter would be too expensive for many company funds. Most funds will still allow existing women members the option of taking their pension early, rather than insisting on their prolonging their working life.

PENSIONS IN PAYMENT

You will have to pay income tax on your pension in the same way as you did on your salary. Public-sector pensions are inflation-proofed and rise every year in line with the Retail Prices Index. Company schemes do not necessarily have this guarantee:

- Some schemes give no guaranteed increases.
- Most funds give a limited guarantee of perhaps 3–4 per cent each year; others have a good track record of giving similar increases but at the discretion of the trustees.
- Legislation is in place but not yet in operation, to increase pensions in payment by 5 per cent per annum, or the rise in the RPI if this is less.
- Trustees of the pension fund have the power to give occasional rises at their discretion if they think pensions are falling too far behind – if only to encourage existing and new members.
- If you are in a final-salary scheme which is contracted out

of SERPs, part of your pension – the guaranteed minimum pension – will increase in line with inflation.

DEATH-IN-RETIREMENT BENEFITS

When a member of a pension fund dies, the surviving spouse will normally qualify for a pension. This is generally half of the employee's pension, although the maximum allowed is two thirds. This applies to both widows and widowers. The payment to the survivor is worked out on the full pension entitlement before any lump sum was deducted. One of the inequitable things about a company pension is that if the employee dies first, the pension is reduced; if the spouse dies first, it stays the same. Most schemes guarantee, however, that if the employee dies during the first five years of retirement, a lump-sum benefit is payable, equal to the pension which would have been paid (at the rate current at the time of death) if the member had lived for the balance of the five years.

ADDITIONAL VOLUNTARY CONTRIBUTIONS (AVCs)

Not many people stay with the same firm all their lives, and we will see in Chapter 6 that job changers generally lose out in terms of accumulated pension when they move from company to company. In addition, you may have joined a pension scheme late in life, which means you will probably not have enough pension entitlement to give you a good standard of living. This is where the AVC comes into play. It enables you to start an additional pension policy of your own to boost your retirement income. But it is important to remember that the longer you defer the decision, the less pension you will have. You need to give your fund a reasonable time to grow.

You can opt either for an in-house scheme run by the company or for a free-standing AVC.

An in-house scheme run by the company

By law every company scheme must offer an AVC plan. The main attraction is that as the employer normally pays all the running costs it offers very good value for money.

A free-standing AVC run by an insurance company

Company AVC schemes are better value, but free-standing policies will sometimes give you a wider investment choice. You can pay into both, subject to the rules listed below, although you can only pay into one free-standing policy in any one tax year.

How an AVC scheme works

Most AVC plans work on the money-purchase basis, which means that the amount you have on retirement to buy a pension will depend on investment performance and how much you pay in. Occasionally an employer will allow you to use an AVC to increase your pension by 'buying' extra years' service instead. The taxman lays down certain rules:

- You can invest up to 15 per cent of your total income, but this must include mainstream pension contributions as well.
- 'Total income' can include not only salary but also bonuses, overtime and the taxable value of any fringe benefits.
- You get tax relief at your top rate of tax on the policy premiums.
- If the premiums paid into a free-standing AVC are less than £2,400 a year, you do not have to tell your employer.
- The earnings 'cap' of £75,000 applies if you joined the company scheme after 1 June 1989.
- You do not have to commit yourself for a fixed period – premiums can generally be varied, both in amount and timing.

- Part of the investment proceeds of policies taken out before 8 April 1987 can be taken in a tax-free lump sum; AVCs which were signed up after that date can only be used to increase your actual pension.
- It is possible to arrange additional life cover through a free-standing policy and get tax relief on the premium.

PENSION PROTECTION

Members of the pension fund have certain rights to information about how the scheme operates and how their pension is building up. Since the Maxwell fraud, there has been new legislation which gives further protection. This includes:

- Basic details of benefits must be given once a year – in practice, good schemes automatically send out an annual benefits statement.
- Transfer-value requests to leave the fund must be sent by your former employer within two months (see Chapter 6).
- Fund trustees must tell members about the Occupational Pensions Advisory Service (OPAS) and the Pensions Ombudsman.
- Trustees must inform fund members if the company is more than three months behind in handing over the members' deducted contributions.

If you belonged to other pension funds before your present job, you will need to keep in touch to find out your pension entitlement. If previous employers have gone bust, OPAS can be helpful in finding out who has taken over responsibility for the funds.

4 Personal Pensions

All about personal pensions for the employed and the self-employed

See also: Chapter 6, Pensions and Job Changers; Chapter 8, Early Retirement

Pensions are all about saving in the most tax-efficient way possible, so that you can enjoy a good standard of living when you retire. Personal pensions fit the bill perfectly.

What is a personal pension?

It is a policy taken out by individuals, both employed and self-employed, where money is invested regularly with an insurance company or other plan provider. The amount of pension you will get at the end of the day depends on how much you pay in and the investment performance of the fund, or funds, you have chosen to invest in. When you decide to retire, you will have a lump sum and this will be used to buy an annuity (see page 101). The annuity will provide your pension for the rest of your life. You do not necessarily have to buy the annuity from the company with which you have been saving (see Chapter 12).

When you take out a policy, you will be given a projection of the likely growth. But remember this is only an estimate and is in no way guaranteed.

Who can buy one?

Basically anyone who pays National Insurance contributions can take out a personal pension. We saw in Chapter 3 that company employees do not have to join the firm's scheme but can have their own personal pension plan instead. This may appeal to younger people who intend changing jobs regularly, as they can take the pension with them. But personal pensions are also suited for:

- employees whose employers do not run a pension scheme
- the self-employed
- people with several sources of income. For example, you may be employed by one company but have separate freelance earnings.

The advantages

A personal pension has the following advantages:

- A state pension alone will not fund a comfortable retirement.
- Tax relief is allowed at your top rate on the premiums.
- The fund grows free of all taxes.
- Retirement age is flexible.
- You have control over your own investments.
- You can take a tax-free lump sum on retirement.
- You can take the pension with you from job to job.
- Up to 5 per cent of your earnings can be used for life insurance.

PERSONAL PENSIONS FOR THE EMPLOYED

If you are an employee, you automatically belong to the government's SERPs scheme unless:

- you 'contract out' via your employer's scheme (see page 21)
- you leave SERPs with the help of a personal pension plan.

Appropriate personal pension

This is the name given to the type of plan used to opt out of SERPs. You and your employer carry on paying the full rate of National Insurance contributions but part – called the rebate – is paid into a personal pension fund. In addition, many people will qualify for a special bonus 'incentive' payment as well. This cash is handed over by the government to the company you choose to run your personal pension. This type of plan is generally called your 'protected rights' and the benefits cannot be taken until state pension age. But how much your protected-rights pension provides depends on how well the invested rebate grows over the years and how much pension your fund will produce at the time you retire.

In effect, the appropriate personal pension is replacing SERPs and the pension will therefore be paid at the same time as the state scheme – age sixty-five for men and sixty for women.

The most important features of the appropriate personal pension are:

- There is no tax-free lump sum with the 'appropriate' pension. It must all go to provide a pension.
- The pension has to be paid on a 'unisex' basis, with the annuity rate being the same for both men and women.
- It must provide a 50 per cent pension for the surviving spouse.
- The pension must increase by 3 per cent each year, or the rise in the Retail Prices Index if this is less.

Contracting out of SERPs in this way is unlikely to be attractive for men over forty-five and women over forty.

The appropriate personal pension plan provides the basics and many younger people may find this sufficient for the present. But older employees need to add on a full-blown personal pension to this basic policy to ensure their retirement income will be sufficient. The rules for personal pensions are broadly the same whether you are employed or self-employed.

PERSONAL PENSIONS FOR THE SELF-EMPLOYED

At least employees with no company pension scheme have SERPs to fall back on – although, as we shall see in the next chapter, that may not be worth a great deal. The self-employed have to make their own pension arrangements if they want to get anything more than the basic state pension. And this is why personal pensions are so beneficial to the self-employed, as well as to employees whose company has no in-house scheme.

Personal pensions in their present form started up in July 1988. Before that, there were old-style self-employed pensions called Section 226 Contracts which are no longer available – more about that later in this chapter.

How much can you invest?

There are limits to what you can pay into your policy every year, and these are based on your age and on your salary or earnings. The older you are, the more you can invest. The maximum contributions are:

Age	Percentage of earnings
up to 35	17.5
36–45	20.0
46–50	25.0
51–55	30.0
56–60	35.0
61–74	40.0

The maximum income which qualifies for a personal pension is currently £75,000. This is revalued every year in line with inflation, in the same way as the company employee's earnings cap (see page 22). For employees, the above percentages are in addition to the rebates you get from National Insurance, which go into the 'appropriate' section of the pension plan.

Premiums

There are two ways you can pay into your policy:

- *Regular premiums.* These can be monthly, quarterly or annual. Most companies will let you increase your payments, for example in line with increased earnings or inflation.
- *Single premiums.* As the name suggests, these are one-off payments made in one lump sum. This gives you the opportunity to reassess your contributions from time to time in line with your finances.

Some regular premium plans will allow you to miss or reduce the occasional payment, although there may be a charge for this. In addition, many policies will have an option to insure for the continuation of payments in the event of sickness.

Tax relief

You get tax relief at your top rate, which means that if you pay tax at 40 per cent, the cost of contributing £100 works out at only £60. If you are self-employed you have to pay the full amount to the insurer and claim back the tax. Employees will get basic-rate tax relief automatically but will have to claim back higher-tax relief from their tax office.

There are two other important tax concessions.

- *Carry forward.* If you have not paid in as much as you are allowed to over the previous six years you can go back over this period to soak up the shortfall.
- *Carry back.* This allows you to have all or part of your pension payments for one tax year to be treated as the previous year's payments. This is useful if you have variable earnings, as it could mean you will pay less tax.

When can you take your pension?

Any time between the ages of fifty and seventy-five. You can carry on working if you want to – there is no need to stop just because you have a pension. For increased flexibility, many people take out several pension plans which allow them to draw the cash and pension at different ages. How much pension you collect depends on the size of your fund, how much you take in a lump sum and the annuity rates prevailing at the time you retire (see Chapter 12).

Lump sum

You can take part of the accumulated pension fund as a tax-free lump sum. This will obviously reduce your pension but normally it will be worthwhile for most people. You can generally take up to 25 per cent of the fund in cash, although your 'protected rights' element mentioned above has to be omitted from the calculation.

Additional life cover

Up to 5 per cent of your earnings can be used to buy life cover for your family. Unlike most insurance premiums this still qualifies for tax relief and can also be used to avoid inheritance tax (see Chapter 9).

TYPES OF PENSION FUND

We have looked at how personal pensions work, but what actually happens to the hard-earned cash which you entrust to the pension provider? Your premiums are invested in different types of pension funds and all of them have a varying degree of risk.

It is as well to remember that your pension is an investment – in fact one of the best examples of long-term investments there is – and that the value may fluctuate over the years. There are four different types of funds.

Unit-linked

All insurers will have a variety of specialist funds on offer in which your premiums are converted into units. These funds cover the whole spectrum of investment, including property, shares quoted on the British and overseas stock markets, and government stocks. The price of the units are quoted in the financial press and you buy them at the offer (higher) price and sell them at the bid (lower) price. The spread between the two prices is normally around 5–6 per cent, which allows for the cost of running the fund. Unit prices will fluctuate according to general economic conditions, stock-market movements and the performance of the fund managers. You can make your own investment decisions by switching from one type of unit to another, although you may attract extra charges if you do this too often.

With-profits

This type of plan can be compared with an endowment policy. Your money goes into the insurance company's general investment pot and is spread between such investments as stocks and shares, government stocks and cash. There is generally a guaranteed growth rate, as well as regular bonuses which go to increase the value.

This investment is not so volatile as unit-linked funds, as part of the profits made in good years are held back to augment performance in the bad times.

Unitized with-profits

This is a recent development which combines features of both of the above funds, but the bonuses will be added on to the price of the units.

Deposit

This is the safest type of investment, as all your contributions are kept in cash and the interest is added on without deduction of tax. This type of fund does not have the potential growth rate of either unit-linking or with-profits. However, it has one very important use. As you near retirement, you will want to have a fair idea of how much you have in your pension kitty. And the last thing you need is for the value of your units to drop through some hiccup in the stock market just when you need them. So a year or two before retirement, it makes sense to come out of your unit fund and move the money into a deposit plan.

DEATH BEFORE RETIREMENT

Should you die before you take your pension, unit-linked and deposit funds will generally pay the value of the accumulated fund to your beneficiaries. Arrangements can be made to ensure that the payment is free of inheritance tax. However, with-profit funds may treat the situation differently: some will return the accumulated value; others will only return your contributions with interest, which is likely to be a lot less than the value of the fund. It is best to find out what is on offer before signing up, especially if you have a family.

And talking of families, it is also possible to arrange to buy a pension for your surviving spouse or other dependants, to cover them if you should die before you retire.

OLD-STYLE SELF-EMPLOYED PENSIONS (SECTION 226 POLICIES)

The self-employed have been able to pay into this type of policy since 1956 but when personal pensions were introduced in 1988, they were withdrawn. However, if you have such a policy, you can either continue with it or switch to the new-style plans. There are basic differences which may influence your thinking:

- *Retirement age.* This is from age sixty to seventy-five as opposed to age fifty to seventy-five for the new style.
- *Amount of pension.* You are not limited to the £75,000

cap as you are with personal pensions, and there are no earnings limits. This will be an important factor for big earners.

- *Lump sum.* The old style generally allows you to take a larger tax-free cash sum when you retire – up to three times the pension you are left with.
- *Limits to what you can invest.* These are less than a personal pension, as the following table shows.

Age	Maximum percentage of earnings
up to 50	17.5
51–55	20.0
56–60	22.5
61–74	27.5

Both types of policies?

If it suits you, you can pay into both types of plans at the same time. The maximum total contributions should not exceed the percentage applicable to your current age for the new-style personal pensions (see page 31). For example, at age fifty-five you can pay up to 30 per cent into a personal pension; if your earnings are £50,000, you can invest up to £15,000, divided between the two types of policy if you prefer.

Big earners – those making more than the £75,000 earnings cap – can get round this limitation by carefully balancing the payments between the two policies.

For example, someone of fifty-five can earn as much as £112,500 and still get full tax relief on the maximum contributions. High earners should take specialist independent advice to ensure that the right steps are taken.

EXECUTIVE PENSIONS

High fliers, company directors and key personnel should seriously consider an executive scheme. There is nothing to stop senior employees from having their own personal pension plan along the lines as described above. However, an executive pension plan has several major advantages:

- An ordinary pension plan is limited by a fixed age percentage. An executive scheme does not have these limits – instead the limit on contributions is only dependent on the benefits that can emerge at retirement.
- The company can pay the bulk of the contributions into the scheme, not the executive.
- There are extremely valuable tax concessions.

An executive scheme has broad similarities to a company scheme (see Chapter 3). These include:

- a pension of up to two thirds final salary at normal retirement age – generally sixty and above
- a tax-free lump sum on retirement
- up to four times salary as a death-in-service benefit
- an automatic spouse's pension.

However there the similarity ends. Much greater amounts can be paid into the executive plan. For example, a man of fifty can invest up to 150 per cent of his earnings at present, although this could be reduced a little in the future. In addition the full two thirds pension can be taken after only twenty years' service (ten years for schemes set up before 17 March 1987), not forty years as is usual with an ordinary company scheme. The twenty years applies to the time as an employee, not as a scheme member.

Executive schemes can be arranged either with an insurance company or set up as a small self-administered scheme (SSAS). The substantial tax advantages include:

- Contributions are allowed against corporation tax.
- Directors pay no tax on the company contributions; at the same time they can also pay in up to 15 per cent of their earnings with top-rate tax relief.
- The pension fund grows free of all taxes.

Executive schemes are complex and specialist advice is an absolute necessity.

5 State Pensions and SERPs

How much you can expect to get from state pensions · whether to contract in or out of SERPs

See also: Chapter 15, Expatriate Pensions

If you have to rely entirely on the state pension for income when you retire, you will certainly be forced to keep to a very strict budget indeed. If you want to enjoy a reasonably comfortable lifestyle in your retirement days, you must make extra provision. It is the difference between fish and chip suppers at home or the occasional night out in a good restaurant.

It is very much part of the government's policy to encourage everyone to make their own private pension arrangements. As a carrot, it gives very valuable tax concessions to persuade as many people as possible to make extra savings for their retirement days. One of the reasons the government is so keen to encourage people to save up for extra pensions is the shifts in population trends. The country is becoming top-heavy with people who have retired – and they are generally much healthier and more active than in previous generations, so they will almost certainly live longer. Great Britain Limited is just not able to generate enough wealth to cater for these rising numbers.

There are two layers of state pension. The first is the basic old-age pension and this is supplemented by the second layer, the State Earnings Related Pension scheme, commonly known as SERPs.

BASIC PENSION

This is derived from your National Insurance contributions and the current maximum single pension is £56.10 per week. To qualify for the full amount, you have to pay NI contributions for about 90 per cent of your working life – which means a contribution record of forty-four years for a man and thirty-nine for a woman.

Important features are:

- The pension is paid weekly and rises each year in line with inflation.
- A man qualifies at age sixty-five, but a woman receives her pension at sixty – although this may change in the future. No early retirement is allowed.
- The pension can be deferred to age seventy for men and sixty-five for women, in return for increased payments.
- Married couples, where one partner is retired and the other not working, receive an extra £33.70 a week.

For most households, this means the maximum basic retirement income will be the princely sum of £89.80 a week. Of course, if both partners qualify for the full state pension, they will each get £56.10 a week.

Not enough stamps?

There are various reasons why you may not have paid enough contributions to qualify for a full basic pension. Perhaps you were abroad or stopped work voluntarily. If you had home responsibilities (see below) or were unemployed your stamps will have been made up automatically.

Whatever the reasons, you do have the chance to fill in the gaps. Currently you can pay a voluntary contribution of £5.45 weekly under Class 3 NI contributions. However, if the gaps were before 1982, you are too late. After that date you have six years to make up the contributions. This could be beneficial to many people nearing retirement as they could then qualify for a full pension rather than a reduced amount.

Ask your DSS for details of how you can pay in extra to improve your contribution record.

SERPs

SERPs is for employees, not the self-employed. Whether you belong to it or not depends on whether your employer operates a scheme which has contracted out of SERPs. But one important principle always applies – if you have not opted out of SERPs, you are a member by default.

You will not belong to SERPs when:

- You have contracted out via a company pension scheme (see page 21). Most company schemes do this, although a small minority still belong to SERPs and run a private pension fund as well.
- You have contracted out by having an appropriate personal pension plan (see Chapter 4).
- You are self-employed.
- Your earnings are below £56 a week, currently the lower earnings limit.

SERPs was first set up in 1978 as an additional pension on top of the basic amount. Since then the amount you can get from the scheme has been reduced. Initially it was designed to provide 25 per cent of earnings over your twenty best years. In future it will only pay 20 per cent of earnings averaged over an employee's working life. These changes won't affect anyone who reaches state pension age before the year 2000. After that the reduced benefits are phased in over ten years. In addition, a spouse can now inherit 50 per cent of a pension, whereas previously a widow could get the full 100 per cent. At present, the maximum anyone retiring shortly can get out of SERPS is around £60 a week, which will not stretch too far! The only good point is that at least SERPs pensions are index-linked.

Limitations to SERPs

The pension does not relate to total earnings. There is an upper and lower limit – currently only income between £56 and £420 weekly qualifies. This means that people earning more than £21,840 a year are wasting pension potential.

No flexibility on retirement age. Men cannot draw the pension before sixty-five and women before sixty. There is no chance of early retirement.

Tax inefficiency. There is no tax relief on your SERPs contributions.

Perhaps the biggest limitation to SERPs is the small amount of pension which it will provide. The scheme should only be regarded as a safety net and you should explore the other options open to you in the field of personal or company pensions.

How much SERPs will you get?

Because of the changes taking place over the next few years, you need to be a mathematical genius to work out the exact figure. However, help is at hand. The Department of Social Security will work out the amount for you, although it may take some time. You need to complete Form BR19, Pension Forecast Application Form (obtainable from the DSS) and send it to the RPFA office at the DSS in Newcastle upon Tyne. This also applies if you need a forecast for your basic state pension.

In or out of SERPs?

In theory, contracting out of SERPs is done every tax year, so you do have the opportunity to go back in if you want. For an employee, the decision will generally depend on the following factors:

- your employer
- your age
- your sex
- how much you can put into a personal pension.

The vast majority of company schemes stay contracted out, so the employee has no choice.

However, if you do not belong to a company scheme, you have the opportunity of leaving SERPs and taking out a personal pension. Much depends on your age and sex, as men and women generally do not benefit equally from SERPs. At present, women retire earlier and live several years longer than men, so they have more to give up. Most insurance companies say that as a general rule it is beneficial for men under forty-five and women under forty to consider leaving SERPs and take a personal pension. If you are older than this, it may be better to stay. However, if your income is above the earnings limits laid down by SERPs, you should be paying extra into a personal plan.

Older employees who are contracted out should consider whether it is worthwhile going back into SERPs as they get nearer retirement. They may still qualify for the higher benefits before the reductions to SERPs mentioned earlier take place.

Appropriate personal pensions

On page 30 we looked at how you can leave SERPs via an appropriate personal pension. The government will pay into your pension plan the NI rebate and in many cases an additional bonus.

However, remember that earnings have to be within the 'band' figures, currently £56 and £420 weekly. This is a good deal for younger people as the pension fund has a long time to grow.

The rebate you are given when you contract out of SERPs was reduced with effect from April 1993 to 4.8 per cent of earnings and the bonus will only be 1 per cent, payable if you are thirty or over. You should take specialist advice according to your individual circumstances.

WOMEN

Special rules apply to state pensions for women – these are spelt out in Chapter 7.

PENSIONS CHECK

This is perhaps a good time to recap on the various combinations of pensions which you can get.

Self-employed

This is the easiest to understand.

- basic state pension
- Section 226, self-employed policy (see page 35)
- personal pension plan.

Employee – member of company scheme contracted out of SERPs

- basic state pension
- company pension
- AVC or FSAVC (see page 26).

Employee – with no company scheme, still belonging to SERPs

- basic state pension
- SERPs pension
- personal pension plan.

Employee – no company scheme, contracted out of SERPs

- basic state pension
- appropriate personal pension
- personal pension plan.

There is nothing to stop you contracting out of SERPs if it is the best option, and continuing with a personal pension as well.

6 Pensions and Job Changers

The pension options when you change jobs · which is best for you

See also: Chapter 3, Pensions for the Employee; Chapter 4, Personal Pensions; Chapter 8, Early Retirement; Chapter 12, Pensions and the Cash Sum

It is quite likely that when you change jobs you will have to decide what to do with a large sum of money. This money never actually gets into your pocket though – you can only get your hands on it when you retire.

But beware – there are predators in the jungle who may want to relieve you of the cash and invest it in their own particular pension plan. Never rush into a decision. This is an area where specialist independent advice is essential, as once you have handed over the money, the decision is irreversible.

Personal pensions and job changers

The beauty of a personal pension is that it is personal to you. You can take it with you from job to job, but at the same time, it can be quite independent of your work. Your employer may contribute to it, although he is not obliged to do so.

There are a few points you should bear in mind:

- If you are redundant or unemployed, and cannot find another job, you cannot continue with the payments, which have to come out of earnings.

- You are allowed to switch your personal pension to another insurance company or other plan provider. However, you should be aware that if you switch or stop a personal pension, there may be extra charges which will reduce the amount of your savings.
- If you belong to a group personal pension plan – basically an umbrella scheme organized for you by your employer – there may also be extra penalties if you leave the scheme or transfer it to another company.
- If your new employer has a company scheme which you decide to join, you will generally not be able to keep the personal pension going. You cannot belong to the employer's scheme and have a personal pension plan at the same time, unless you have other non-pensionable earnings.

CHOICES FOR JOB CHANGERS

The chart opposite shows the various choices open to you for rethinking your pension when you change jobs. It probably looks confusing at first glance but we'll take you through the various stages so that you will be able to consider all the options.

The vast majority of job changers who belong to a pension fund are in a final-salary scheme (see page 20) and the following is based on that assumption.

Take a refund

You can only have a refund if you have belonged to the scheme for less than two years.

- You will have to pay 20 per cent tax on the refund, which has hitherto had the benefit of tax relief.
- Only your own contributions are refunded.
- You can take out a personal pension plan with the refund to cover your last two years' earnings.
- If you were contracted out of SERPSs, part of the refund will be used to buy you back into the state scheme.

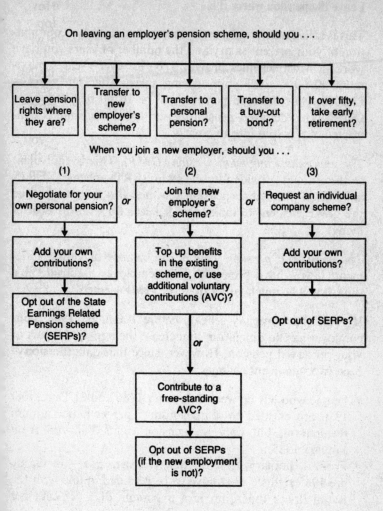

On leaving an employer's pension scheme, should you . . .

| Leave pension rights where they are? | Transfer to new employer's scheme? | Transfer to a personal pension? | Transfer to a buy-out bond? | If over fifty, take early retirement? |

When you join a new employer, should you . . .

(1)   (2)   (3)

Negotiate for your own personal pension?   *or*   Join the new employer's scheme?   *or*   Request an individual company scheme?

Add your own contributions?

Top up benefits in the existing scheme, or use additional voluntary contributions (AVC)?

Add your own contributions?

Opt out of the State Earnings Related Pension scheme (SERPs)?

or

Opt out of SERPs?

Contribute to a free-standing AVC?

Opt out of SERPs (if the new employment is not)?

The Transfer Maze

Source: Towry Law Group.

Leave the pension where it is

This is called a deferred pension; it is calculated on a combination of your present salary and the number of years you have worked. Most schemes provide 1/60 for every year – maximum 40/60 – so if your leaving salary after ten years is £30,000, your deferred pension will be 10/60 of £30,000, or £5,000. This deferred pension (assuming the scheme is contracted out) is split into two parts:

The guaranteed minimum pension (GMP). This is equivalent to the amount provided by the state SERPs scheme. SERPs is inflation-proofed so pension schemes also have to revalue the GMP element to make sure it keeps up with the cost of living.

The non-GMP pension. This is the balance of your entitlement; if you have been with your employer a considerable time, it will be much larger than the GMP element.

If you left a company scheme before 1 January 1986, your employer has no obligation to increase the non-GMP part of your preserved pension. However, since that date there have been two significant changes:

- People who left between 1 January 1986 and 31 December 1990 are entitled to a maximum 5 per cent per annum revaluation, but only on pension rights built up from January 1985.
- From 1 January 1991 all deferred pensions – including pre-1985 rights – now have to be revalued in line with the Retail Prices Index, up to a maximum of 5 per cent per annum.

This is a step in the right direction, but it is still likely that when you come to draw a deferred pension you will lose out, as earnings normally rise faster than inflation. If you stay with an employer until retirement, the £5,000 mentioned in the above example is likely to increase at a far greater rate than the deferred pension.

Transfer your pension

You do not have to leave your pension with your previous company. Since 1 January 1986, job changers have had the right to be given a 'transfer value' of their accumulated pension and take it away from the employer (though not within one year of normal retirement age). The transfer value is the cash lump sum which an actuary estimates to be the equivalent of the deferred pension described above. Interest rates also influence the final amount. Generally the lower the market rates, the more transfer value you get – and vice versa.

The cash never gets into your pocket. It has to be transferred from the pension fund to one of three choices:

- your new employer's scheme, if there is one
- a personal pension plan
- an insurance company bond, called a Section 32 buy-out plan.

You can ask the pensions department for a transfer value at any time and, under recent legislation, they must respond within two months. The figure is worked out taking current interest rates into account, and the quotation will be valid for a set period – perhaps three or six months.

New employer's scheme

You could be in for a bit of a shock here. For a start, a new employer is not obliged to accept the transfer into his scheme. And if he does agree, you will almost certainly find that the number of years' service you can buy into the new scheme will be a lot less than the actual years you have worked.

If we look at the example on page 48, the deferred pension of £5,000 after ten years' service would have a transfer value of, say, £25,000. This sum could be invested in the new employer's scheme, but he may only be prepared to let you have the rights to six years' service, not the ten which you have actually worked.

The reasoning behind this is that your salary on retirement is likely to be a lot higher than your salary on leaving a former employer. If you were allowed the full ten years on retirement under a final salary scheme, your actual pension would be much higher than the £5,000 which you have earned so far. But you have only paid in enough transfer cash to buy £5,000 worth of pension, so to balance this you are credited with fewer years' service.

Personal pension plan

The transfer value of £25,000 can be invested in a personal pension plan. Lump sums from contracted-out schemes have to be split into two parts in the same way as a deferred pension. One part, representing the guaranteed minimum pension, goes into an appropriate personal pension (described on page 30). These are known as protected rights. The word 'protected' can cause some confusion. The benefits have to be protected – for example there has to be a spouse's pension as well as inflation-proofing. However, the amount of the pension is not guaranteed and depends on the investment performance of the pension fund and the annuity rates prevailing at retirement.

The second part of the transfer value is what is left over after the GMP has been dealt with and it operates along the same lines as an ordinary personal pension. This allows you a flexible retirement age, a tax-free lump sum and the other benefits described on page 29.

As with all personal pensions, this will be a money-purchase scheme, which means that your cash is put into a range of investments. How much pension you get on top of the protected-rights element depends on how well these investments grow.

Section 32 buy-out bond

These schemes were first introduced in 1981. Once again the
pension is divided into two parts, consisting of the guaranteed
minimum pension and the excess. With a buy-out bond, the
GMP slice is guaranteed and in some cases can even be
taken before state retirement age. The excess amount is
invested in much the same way as a personal pension.

Buy-out bonds can be good for older employees because of
the guaranteed pension. They can sometimes provide large
amounts of tax-free cash.

WHAT'S THE BEST CHOICE FOR YOU?

The biggest problem is that it is very difficult to compare one
with another. The choices you are offered when you leave an
employer all have good and not-so-good points, depending
on your personal circumstances. That is why it is essential to
talk to the experts and not rush into a decision.

Above all, you need to understand the risks involved. By
leaving your pension with a previous employer, you know
exactly where you stand and you have some protection
against inflation. However, if inflation increases beyond 5
per cent, the purchasing power of your fixed pension will be
eroded.

On the other hand, the longer you can leave your money in
a personal pension or a buy-out bond, the better your chances
of building up a fund which will provide a larger pension –
and one which will stay ahead of inflation. But you should
remember that the size of the pension depends on investment
performance.

Much will depend on your age, marital status and temperament.

- If you move jobs close to retirement, it is probably better
  to leave your pension with your ex-employer.
- If you still have about ten years or so to go, there is a lot

of merit in a Section 32 buy-out, because of the guarantees involved.

- Single people generally get a better deal out of a personal pension, as they do not have to use any of the fund to buy a pension for a spouse.
- If the pension is going to be the major part of your retirement income, you have to decide whether you want to take the investment risks of an insurance policy or the safety of your previous employer's scheme.

INCREASED TRANSFER VALUE

There are changes in the law on the horizon which for many people could mean an increased transfer value, which will improve overall benefits. This is a very good reason why you should not be persuaded to sign up with the first pensions adviser who crosses your threshold. Take independent advice first, as a hasty decision could mean the loss of substantial future income for ever.

7 Women, Pensions and Divorce

Why women have different pensions provision from men · what they should do to ensure a fair deal on divorce

See also: Chapter 3, Pensions for the Employee; Chapter 4, Personal Pensions; Chapter 5, State Pensions and SERPs

Women have different pension provision from men because they tend to live longer and retire earlier, and they are more likely to take career breaks when they have children or to look after relatives.

Women fare badly in the pension stakes. According to the Equal Opportunities Commission, only 15 per cent of women in Britain can claim the full state pension in their own right – many still have to rely on their husband's pension. Retired married women drawing a pension in their own right get only £36 on average a week, compared with the full pension of £56.10.

Women are the poor relations in private pension schemes as well. Although 60 per cent of men belong to a company pension scheme, less than 40 per cent of working women are members and they draw much smaller pensions. The average company pension payment for a man between the ages of fifty-five and sixty-nine is £61 weekly, compared with only £30 for women.

Generally women retire earlier than men, but live longer – on average five to six years longer. By the end of this century it is expected that women will have an average life expectancy of nearly eighty years compared with seventy-four years for men.

PENSION DIFFICULTIES FACED BY WOMEN

- Women earn less than men and often find it harder to put aside a regular sum to pay into a pension plan.
- As most company pension schemes and SERPS are salary-linked, women whose earnings are lower get lower pensions.
- More than two million women are paid less than the lower earnings limit, now £56 a week, so don't qualify for the state pension scheme at all.
- One out of every three marriages ends in divorce and in these circumstances women often don't get a fair share of their husband's pension rights.
- Since 1978 women have had the same right as men to join the company pension scheme, but part-time workers are often excluded – and the majority of these are women.
- Women are more likely to work for employers that do not provide a pension scheme.
- As women live longer than men and can therefore expect to go on drawing a pension for longer, they have to pay more for comparable pensions. It is estimated that a woman of twenty-five will have to pay 10 per cent more than a man to a pension scheme in order to buy the same yearly pension.

State pensions for women

Plans are now being made to equalize the retirement age, although no fixed date or ages have yet been set. However, given the vast cost of providing state pensions, it is likely that the retirement age for women will be raised to sixty-five rather than the age for men being lowered to sixty. It is also expected that the change will be phased in, so that women in their fifties now won't be too badly affected.

There are special rules which apply to state pensions for women:

- Women who have worked all their lives will get the full basic pension at age sixty. If they have only worked for part of their working lives, they can still qualify for a reduced pension in their own right.
- Married women who have never worked will get a pension based on their husband's contributions. However a wife must be over sixty to claim this and at the same time her husband must be sixty-five or over, and retired.
- Under independent taxation, a wife can now have her share of the pension set off against her own allowances, which should reduce tax liability for many couples.
- Home responsibilities protection (HRP) – National Insurance contributions are covered by the state for anyone who stays at home to look after a child or an elderly relation (unless you are being paid Invalid Care Allowance). This means pension rights are safeguarded.
- Many women retiring today or within the next few years have been paying reduced-rate contributions. The cost is usually lower than paying the full rate, but they won't qualify for a basic pension in their own right and will have to rely on their husbands' contributions.

What steps you can take

- Get an estimate from the DSS of how much basic state pension you will be able to claim – all you need to do is to complete form BR19, available from local DSS offices. In order to get the full pension you need to work for thirty-nine years – and not many women manage to achieve that record. You can pay voluntary Class 3 contributions of £5.45 a week, which will protect your basic state pension rights (not SERPs) during the periods when you are not employed and do not qualify for HRP (see above) or unemployment benefit.
- Make sure you are paying the full-rate National Insurance contributions. Until 1977 married women could opt to pay a reduced-rate National Insurance – known as the 'small

stamp' – and those paying the reduced rate could carry on paying at the lower level for as long as they liked, or until retirement. Today as many as two million women pay this reduced amount. It nearly always makes economic sense to switch over to paying the full rate – ask your DSS office for more information. Once you've moved to the full rate, you cannot switch back.

- If you have earnings from employment and don't belong to a company pension scheme you will be a member of the State Earnings Related Pension scheme – known as SERPs. Get an estimate of how much you can expect to be paid from this source as well.

- Think seriously about taking out a personal pension plan – talk to an independent financial adviser, who will suggest suitable policies. It is never too late to start saving up for retirement and even if you only have a few years to go it is still worth starting up a plan to give you extra cash when you are no longer working.

- Husbands who are self-employed, or run their own businesses, often pay their wives a small salary to do 'secretarial and admin. work' for them. Women in this position should consider putting some of this cash into a personal pension plan.

- If you are a member of a company pension scheme, think seriously about paying into the top-up scheme known as Additional Voluntary Contributions or AVCs for short (see Chapter 3). However, the schemes are usually more expensive for women than men because of the longer life expectancy. The life company involved assumes that women will be drawing the pension for longer, so pays out less, even when the pension is to be paid out at the same age. One company quoted an annual payout of £120 per £1,000 of pension cash for a man aged sixty, but for a woman of the same age the payout was £112.

PENSIONS AND DIVORCE

One out of every three marriages now ends in divorce. What this means for the woman is that she loses all rights to any widow's pension paid by the state or by her former husband's employer. A divorced woman has no entitlement to her husband's SERPs pension, but she can claim a pension in respect of her former spouse's basic state pension entitlement.

If the woman subsequently remarries, her entitlement to the state pension will be based on her current husband's record – unless she is sixty-plus at the time of remarriage. In this case, her state pension entitlement is based on her former husband's record and can't be taken away from her.

Although pension rights are one of the most valuable assets built up by a couple during a marriage, in England and Wales there are no strict rules about what should happen to them on divorce. In Scotland the situation is different – the value of pension rights must be taken into account when matrimonial assets are split, although the pension rights stay with the contributing member.

The leading pensions organization, the National Association of Pension Funds, has called for the government to introduce rules to allow wives to obtain a share of their ex-husband's pension on divorce. Pension rights would be evaluated at the time of the divorce and then split on a 50/50 basis, though if the marriage has lasted for less than two years, or less than £5,000 is at stake, they can still be ignored.

However, it is likely to be several years before any action is taken, and in the meantime it is essential for marriage partners who are splitting up to take the pension benefits into account when working out who gets what. It is possible for an actuary, or even the pension-fund managers, to value pension rights which have been built up at a specified date. The actual value is discounted to allow for the time lapse before the pension is actually drawn.

Women often sacrifice their careers to raise a family and in the process greatly lessen the amount of pension they will get at retirement age. Lawyers are often not as informed on pension rights as they should be and have been known to overlook them completely when working out divorce settlements. It is best to go to a specialist family-law solicitor and to make sure they know about pension rights and are taking them into account when calculating the divorce settlement.

8 Early Retirement

How much pension you can draw if you retire early · what you can do to boost your income

See also: Chapter 3, Pensions for the Employee; Chapter 5, State Pensions and SERPs; Chapter 12, Pensions and the Cash Sum

The options for early retirement have increased enormously over the last few years.

- Personal pension plans can be drawn from the age of fifty onwards.
- The 1989 Budget agreed that employees could draw a full pension from the age of fifty, provided that they had been with their employer for at least twenty years. A woman can retire at age forty-five provided she is within ten years of the company's retirement age.
- You do not actually have to give up working when you retire. You can still draw your pension and find another job – perhaps part-time if this suits you better.

So the opportunity to give up work early is there – but will you have enough money to take advantage of it? Most people will probably need other income or capital to take early retirement in their fifties, as the amount of pension they have earned will not be sufficient to live on comfortably. There are penalties for early retirement, simply because the pension will have to be paid for longer. And you always have to remember that a pension fund of any sort needs time to grow.

STATE PENSIONS

Do not expect any help from the state. The state is totally inflexible and both basic and SERPs pensions cannot be drawn until the official retirement age – currently sixty for women and sixty-five for men (see Chapter 5).

- If you do retire early, your basic pension may be reduced because you will not have paid enough stamps. To ensure you get the full pension you will have to pay voluntary Class 3 contributions until retirement age.
- If you are forced to retire early because of ill health, you qualify for Invalidity Benefit. How much you get depends on your age and National Insurance contributions.

COMPANY PENSIONS

Generally, early retirement comes in one of three ways:

- enforced, such as redundancy or company closure
- voluntary, where the company is looking to reduce the workforce and calls for volunteers
- requested, where you ask to retire early.

More and more employees are having to face the problem of early retirement because of redundancy. If your employer is generous, you should be able to get a package which includes your full pension entitlement to date, or even a full pension if you are very near to retirement. This will tend to ease the hardship of enforced early retirement.

The rules for early retirement are set out by the taxman. If you retire voluntarily before the normal retirement age of your pension fund, the Inland Revenue says that your pension must be scaled down accordingly, although there is some flexibility.

- The earliest you can take a pension is generally at the age of fifty.
- Under a final-salary scheme, you normally qualify for one

sixtieth of your final salary for every year worked, up to
the date you take early retirement.
- The tax-free lump sum is also usually scaled down.

If the offer is made by the company, you can expect a
pension and lump sum worked out on your final salary to
date, in relation to the number of years' service. This is not
necessarily automatic and your pension could be reduced if
the offer from your employer is not particularly generous. All
parts of the pension can be paid immediately, including the
bit attributable to contracting out of SERPs.

If you yourself ask to go early, you normally have to get
agreement from the scheme's trustees. Assuming they agree,
you are likely to find that the scheme makes substantial
reductions in the amount of pension it is prepared to pay.

This is decided on the basis that your pension will have to
be paid over a longer period than normally expected. It is
often called an 'actuarial reduction' and can be 6–8 per cent
for every year before normal retirement age. As the table
below shows, someone retiring at fifty with a normal retirement age of sixty-five could find themselves with only a
fraction of the pension they expected.

Number of years in scheme	Age at early retirement			
	50	55	60	63
	Percentage of expected pension that will be paid			
10	14	24	42	72
20	19	33	56	78
30	25	37	60	81

The above percentages are based on one sixtieth of final
salary for each year in the scheme with a compounded
actuarial reduction of $7\frac{1}{2}$ per cent and the assumption that
normal salary would have increased by 5 per cent every year.
This is a typical example, but schemes will vary. However, it
does show that early retirement for employees is not feasible
unless a great deal of forward financial planning takes place.

Money-purchase pension

If your company has a money-purchase scheme – one where investment growth decides the amount of your fund – your situation is similar to that of someone with an ordinary personal pension.

Ill health

The taxman's rules are much more generous if you have to retire because of ill health. There is no age restriction and the company can pay a full pension based on your normal retirement age if its rules permit.

PERSONAL PENSIONS

A personal pension plan allows retirement at age fifty onwards. The old-style Section 226 self-employed policies limited retirement age to sixty. However:

- You are allowed to transfer an old-style pension to a new personal pension plan.
- This allows you to retire before the age of sixty.
- You will then be subject to the rules for personal pensions, which could reduce your tax-free lump sum (see Chapter 4).

The good news is that there are no limits to what you can draw under a personal pension. The earnings cap of £75,000 only applies to the contributions. However, if you decide to retire early, the pension will be lower because:

- You will have paid in less in contributions. The percentage you can invest increases as you get older.
- Your fund will have had less time to grow.
- You will get lower annuity rates. These are fully described on page 101; they work on the principle that the younger you are the less you will get.

- The pension plan may have a surrender penalty if it is cashed in early.
- You can still take part of your fund as a tax-free lump sum.
- The same points also apply to a company employee moncy-purchase scheme and an AVC.

The table below shows the estimated pension as a percentage of present-day earnings which could be earned assuming you have been investing 15 per cent of your income for the time shown. Once again it is only a guide, as plans will vary.

Male aged	Age at retirement			
	50	55	60	63
	Pension as a percentage of earnings			
25	35	47	63	75
30	27	37	51	62
35	19	28	40	49
40	12	20	31	39
45	6	13	21	29

These percentages assume a 10 per cent per annum compounded increase in income and 13 per cent growth in investments. The figures for a woman will be marginally lower. A 50 per cent spouse's pension has been provided and pensions are assumed to increase at 3 per cent a year.

Ill health

If you are forced to retire because of ill health, you can generally take your pension at any age. However, the above points still apply – you may not have enough in the pot to make it worthwhile. You can protect your contributions by taking out a 'waiver of premium' insurance. This allows the policy to grow normally, even if premiums are not being made because you are too ill to work. There will be an extra charge for this benefit.

WHAT CAN YOU DO ABOUT IT?

The answer is simple – plan ahead and start as soon as you can. The execution may not be so simple, as it all depends on having the income available. But for a company scheme member with limited years of service it means taking out AVCs or free-standing AVCs. For the self-employed and those not in a company scheme it means taking advantage of the maximum percentage allowances which can be placed in a personal pension – these increase with age (see Chapter 4).

Everyone with early retirement in mind should take advantage of all the other tax-efficient investments available so that, when the day comes, you have enough of a financial cushion to recline on. These include National Savings certificates, TESSAs and Personal Equity Plans (see Chapter 2).

Phased retirement

For the self-employed – and anyone else with a personal pension – the answer could be to phase in your retirement over a number of years. This means a series of plans spread over a number of years so that you can gradually draw an ever-increasing pension. Remember that there is no need to stop full-time or part-time work simply because you are receiving a pension.

One of the most efficient ways is to have a policy which is 'segmented' into a number of mini-policies – perhaps a hundred in all. This is extremely tax efficient, as it allows sufficient income every year, together with tax-free cash. At the same time, the rest of the fund is left to grow totally tax free. There are also other benefits:

- In the event of early death, a pension can be lost for ever. If there is a balance in your fund, this will go to your family.
- There is potential for a higher pension over the years. The

older you are when you cash in part of your fund, the greater the pension annuity (see Chapter 12).
- Your tax bill is reduced as you can take tax-free cash every time you take out a 'segment'.

9 Wills and Inheritance Tax Planning

What happens if you die without a will · will forms · will-writing agencies · solicitors · writing a will · inheritance tax rules – how to plan, what is tax free · Deed of Variation · inheritance tax insurance

See also: Chapter 22, When Someone Dies

It is a known fact that writing a will does not kill you – nor hasten your death. Yet two out of three people in this country don't have wills – many because subconsciously they fear that the act of writing one might tempt fate. And since there are no pockets in shrouds, there may be a case to be made for saying that it doesn't matter to you what happens to your money when you pass on. However, people do want to have a say in the dividing up of their cash – even if it is only to stop someone they don't like getting their sticky fingers on the money they worked so hard to amass.

INTESTATE

If you die intestate – without a will – then the state divides up your money. The rules are laid down as to how this is done, and who gets what depends on what immediate family you have. But the division is different in Scotland to what it is in England and Wales. There is one similarity. Contrary to popular opinion, if you are not married your partner gets nothing. Under English law there is no such thing as a common-law wife or common-law husband, so even if you have lived together for twenty years the surviving partner won't inherit anything because they are not family. The rules are almost as strict in Scotland. So if you cohabit it is doubly important to have a properly written will.

There can be another problem too. If all of a family's money is in, say, the husband's name and he dies, then the wife will have no way of gaining access to that cash until after probate. That means she won't be able to pay bills unless she borrows the money to do so. And although a bank may be very sympathetic to her case and lend her a lump sum against her likely inheritance, she'll have to pay interest on the money. If you have a will, probate is usually much quicker.

WRITING A WILL

There are three alternatives when it comes to writing your will. Which one you use depends on how much you can afford, and how complicated your affairs are:

- DIY
- will-writing agency
- solicitor.

DIY

Writing a will need not be expensive. It can cost as little as a fiver or so if you buy a will form from a newsagent's, follow the instructions and fill it in yourself. That may be alright if your affairs really are very simple, or you cannot afford to go to a solicitor, but it is not the recommended route for most people. You can get it very wrong. Like the man who wrote on his form that he left '£1,000 to my next-door neighbour'. By the time of his death, however, the neighbour had moved away, and got nothing; the new neighbours played loud music all day and were unfriendly – but inherited £1,000.

But if your affairs are very simple and you follow the instructions carefully, you will probably be alright with one of these forms.

> **Tip**
> If you are buying a will form, remember to buy the right form for the country you live in: a Scottish form for those living in Scotland and an English one for those living in England and Wales, so that you follow the instructions appropriate for the law of the country in which you live.

Will-writing agency

A halfway house is to use one of the will-writing agencies. They will charge a bit more – usually between £20 and £30 – but your will is usually checked by a lawyer to make sure that it is legally correct. It is worth making sure, if you are using one of these services, that a lawyer will in fact be looking over the will. A drawback here is that these services often come with plenty of advice for other financial products you might like to buy. Stand your ground and don't buy what you don't need or want.

> **Tip**
> If you can't afford a solicitor, write your will yourself on a DIY form, keep it simple and then take it along to your local Citizens Advice Bureau. They often have legal clinics or helpful solicitors who will be prepared to check your will free of charge.

Solicitor

Most solicitors would tell you that they don't make much money writing a will. Most charge around £30–40 for a simple, straightforward will, and around £75 for a married couple. But the more complicated your affairs are the more they will charge. If you need trusts to be set up or have a lot of legacies to leave it could cost a lot more. What you pay depends on how much of the solicitor's time you take up. Imagine a taxi meter running in the lawyer's office – the longer you are in there the more it will cost. So, to keep the bill low, make sure you know exactly what you want to

leave, and to whom, before you arrive. Have names and
addresses written down and a very clear idea in your mind of
what you want to say and it shouldn't cost you much more
than a car service.

Tip
Always use a solicitor if your affairs are complicated or you
want to set up a trust.

What you need to know

Before you write a will you need to have certain details
at your fingertips. Whether you are using a solicitor or doing
it yourself, it is worthwhile getting organized first.

Testator – that's you. Your name and address has to go on
the will.

Executors – the person or people who carry out your
instructions. Remember to ask them first because not everyone welcomes this job. And it is a good idea to choose
someone your own age or younger so that they are still alive
when you die. If your affairs are complicated you might like
to choose a friend or relative as one of the executors and a
professional – either your lawyer or the bank – as the other.
But, of course, the professional will charge for this service. A
bank's bill tends to depend on the value of the estate, a
lawyer's on the amount of time that is put in. Either way, the
estate pays the bill before the money is distributed to your
heirs. If the will is straightforward your executors may not
need the help, or the cost, of a professional.

Beneficiaries – that's the people who get your money. You
can either pay them amounts of money, i.e. '£2,000 to my
son John Jones', or a percentage of the estate, i.e. '50 per
cent of the total to my son John Jones'. Or you can leave
gifts – 'my car to my godson William Smith'.

You'll need full names and addresses of all beneficiaries

and it helps if you put down their relationship to you as well – even if it is only 'James Grant, my next-door neighbour, who lives at . . .'

Estate – that's what you leave. It may be your house, car, proceeds of life-insurance policies, shares, building society account, premium bonds, wine cellar, antique table, whatever. All your assets are added together, any debts you have are taken off and what remains is your estate.

Bequests – the little gifts you want to make. Any personal items you want to go to specific people – your jewellery to your daughter, or your bowls to your bowling partner – should be detailed clearly. If you are leaving any money to a charity it is important that you get the name and address correct or they may not get the bequest.

Dying together – your will should have a clause outlining what you want to happen to your money should a husband and wife die together, or indeed if the parents and children are all killed in one accident. If you don't, then the estate will be divided up according to the intestacy rules – which may or may not suit you.

Cutting someone out. In England and Wales you can leave your money to whosoever you choose – providing that your financial dependants are taken care of first. A wife or child, or stepchild, who relies on you for their upkeep – that is, someone who is financially dependent on you in life – must be catered for before you go ahead and leave everything to Fulham Football Club. In Scotland it is not so easy to cut someone out. Your spouse and all your children have a legal right to a percentage of your estate, regardless of your relationship with them on your death. Just because you haven't spoken to your son for forty-five years does not mean you can cut him out of your will.

Signing the will. No will is valid unless it is properly signed and witnessed. The witness should not be a beneficiary of the will (or they will lose their legacy), an executor or blind. The two witnesses must see the will being signed and then sign it themselves in front of each other – but they do not have to see the contents of the will.

In Scotland, if the will is handwritten (a holograph will) and signed then the signature does not need to be witnessed.

Codicil – an alteration to your will. If you want to make a simple change to your will you can do so by adding a paragraph at the end, after the signatures and witnesses. This is known as a codicil and it has to be properly witnessed, in the same way as the will, by two independent signatories.

Revoking the will

Once your will has been made it will stand, in law, unless you make another one or you get married. Marriage automatically revokes your will (though not in Scotland) and if you don't make a new one on marriage, you will be deemed to have died intestate. And of course any bequests that you made would be lost. North of the border, marriage does not revoke your will, but your spouse won't be included in the will. So unless you make a new will, or your spouse claims what is legally theirs, they will miss out on any of your estate.

Divorce, on the other hand, does not revoke a will. It will cut out the claims of a former spouse, but your bequests and other legacies will still stand.

Will Trust

You can draw up your will in such a way that you leave your spouse an income for life but on death the capital passes to your children. You do it by setting up a Will Trust, and you'll need professional help.

INHERITANCE TAX PLANNING

Hand in hand with writing a will goes inheritance tax planning. It is not a tax you ever pay on your own money – it is paid by your heirs – so theoretically you needn't bother to cut the bill. But if you worked hard for your money, you may not want to see it slipping easily and quietly into the coffers of the Revenue. And a few simple steps taken while you are alive will cut the bill drastically when you die.

What is inheritance tax?

Inheritance tax is the swipe that the taxman makes at your estate before you pass it on. When you die your estate is valued. The first £150,000 that you leave is free of all tax: anything above that is taxed at 40 per cent:

> under £150,000 – no tax paid
> above £150,000 – tax at 40 per cent.

This rule assumes that you have not made any gifts of money in the last seven years of your life.

The inheritance tax threshold is raised in most Budgets to keep it at least in line with inflation. And the Conservative government may do something to ease the burden of this tax: John Major is on record as saying that he wants wealth to 'cascade down the generations'. But until new legislation is on the statute book there is plenty you can do to ensure that as much of your money as possible flows in the direction of your heirs.

Outplanning the taxman

It would seem quite simple to outwit the Inland Revenue by giving all but £150,000 of your money away on your deathbed so that there is nothing left to tax, but it is not as simple as that.

The seven-year rule

After you make any gift, you have to live for seven years to avoid paying inheritance tax on it. So you can, for example, give away £10,000 to a child, but if you don't then live for another seven years that sum will be taken into the inheritance tax calculations.

But the full 40 per cent tax may not have to be paid. The Inland Revenue uses the following scale when working out what tax is due:

Years between gift and death	Percentage of tax payable
up to 3	100
3–4	80
4–5	60
5–6	40
6–7	20
7 or more	0

If you live for seven years after you have made the gift then it will be free of all inheritance tax. But don't try to fool the taxman by pretending to give something away which you haven't, or by keeping an interest in it. For example, you can't give your godchild the £10,000 you have in the building society but still have the interest paid to you; or give your house to your children but continue to live in it rent-free. A gift is just that – something you give away completely.

When you don't pay inheritance tax

There are times when you can give away money and not pay inheritance tax on it. They are quite specific occasions and the main ones are listed below.

No inheritance tax will be paid if the gift:

- is between husband and wife.
- totals no more than £3,000 a year. You can carry this allowance forward for one tax year, but only one year.
- is less than £250. You can give as many tranches of £250

as you like so long as they are to different people and don't go to the same people as got the £3,000. The £250 tranches don't count towards the £3,000 in any way as they are a separate allowance.

- is a wedding present. The parent of the bride and groom can give up to £5,000; a grandparent or great-grandparent can give £2,500; anyone else can give £1,000.
- is part of a divorce settlement (if done before the divorce).
- is to support a widowed, divorced or separated mother or mother-in-law, any other old or infirm relative or handicapped child.
- is to a UK charity.
- is to a UK political party which must have at least two MPs.

Also free of inheritance tax at death are:

- certain works of art and woodlands
- agricultural land or business assets and unquoted shares, if eligible for 100 per cent relief
- your funds at Lloyd's within reasonable limits.

And that's it. Anything else comes under the inheritance tax umbrella and is subject to the seven-year rule. But you can still reduce your bill substantially with a little forethought.

Plan a reduced bill

There are several steps you can take now – and one or two that your heirs can take – that will substantially reduce the taxman's cut of your estate.

- If you are rich enough, give away up to £150,000 and live for seven years, and then you can give away more.
- Use up your £3,000 and £250 exemptions, every year – and remember that your £3,000 gift can be carried forward for one year, so if you didn't use it in the last tax year you can do so now.
- Remember that a couple each have their own exemptions,

which doubles the £3,000 and £250 inheritance-tax-free gifts.

- Use the exemption which allows you 'normal expenditure out of income' to fund a life-insurance policy in trust for your children or grandchildren, or anyone else.
- Watch your will. If you think your spouse will be comfortably enough off without needing your entire estate, start to pass some of your cash down a generation. That way you will reduce the bill.

Example 1

Norma Jones dies leaving £300,000. Her will passes it all to her husband Gordon. No inheritance tax is paid because the money passes from one spouse to the other.

A year later Gordon dies. The money passes to his son and the inheritance tax bill is:

> £150,000 . . . no tax
> £150,000 . . . taxed at 40 per cent
> tax bill . . . £60,000

This whole bill could have been avoided by one simple move.

Example 2

Norma Jones dies leaving £300,000. Half goes to her husband Gordon and the other half to her son. No inheritance tax is paid because the money going to her son is below the inheritance tax threshold.

A year later Gordon dies. The money – £150,000 – passes to his son. No inheritance tax is paid, so the son saves £60,000 which would otherwise have gone to the Inland Revenue.

Splitting up the house

It makes a difference how the house is owned.
You either own it as:

- joint tenants
- tenants in common.

Joint tenants – this means the survivor owns the whole house. Tenants in common – this means you each own one half share and you can dispose of it in your will any way you want. This can allow you to make use of your nil rate band but it may cause family frictions if your spouse ends up having to sell the house in order to give the children their share.

Check the deeds of your house to see which way you own your home, and make the appropriate changes through your solicitor, if necessary.

Deed of Variation

Up to two years after a death, the heirs can apply for what is known as a Deed of Variation to rewrite the provisions of the will. Provided they all agree, they could change the terms, usually to make a tax saving. So Norma's will could have been altered to turn it from the original terms in Example 1 to the tax-saving terms of Example 2.

But be warned. The Inland Revenue has already had one go at getting rid of the Deed of Variation. It was saved at the last minute, but might not be next time, so don't rely on it. Change your will now.

Insuring against an inheritance tax bill

If you don't want to give your money away now or worry that you may not live for seven years after you have, there is an additional course of action you can take. Insure against the bill.

If you are giving away at least £150,000 now but fear dying before the seven-year rule wipes out the tax bill, what you need is term insurance. You will be able to work out how much a likely inheritance tax bill is – and of course it reduces every year that you live – so it is quite easy to buy a policy that will cover the bill. Remember that the proceeds should be paid to the beneficiaries, not into your estate or you will increase rather than reduce the likely inheritance tax bill.

Example

A seventy-year-old man gives £300,000 to his daughter. The inheritance tax bill if he dies within twelve months is £60,000 reducing to £12,000 if he dies in year six.

Term insurance would cost around £130 a month for six years (though it provides cover for the whole seven years because no tax is paid in the final year) and if this is paid out of normal income it would be inheritance tax free. Or you could pay a single premium of £7,000 but, ironically, this would be treated as a gift too! One way round this would be for his daughters to pay the £7,000.

If the seventy-year-old man lives for the seven years, the premium money would be lost; if he dies, the policy would pay out to cover the tax bill.

Under-seventies

If you are still under seventy, you can insure against an inheritance tax bill by buying a life insurance policy. On your death it pays out a lump sum – which should match the likely inheritance tax bill – so that although the bill is still presented by the Inland Revenue, your heirs have the funds to pay it from the life insurance policy.

Don't go for the usual with-profits policy; move instead towards a low-cost or unit-linked policy that will offer a high level of life cover more quickly. It won't build in value as substantially as a with-profits policy, but what you need at this stage is a quick start. A man of sixty with a wife of fifty-seven wanting to cover a likely bill of £100,000 would pay monthly premiums of around £140, paying out when the survivor dies – and when the tax bites.

Over-seventies

Once you breach seventy, life insurance is just too expensive to buy. You will need something a bit more financially sophisticated. But if your estate is worth more than £300,000 it is worth persevering to understand what you must do. What you need is known as a 'back-to-back' policy. To cover your potential inheritance tax liability, you need an insurance policy which will pay out a lump sum on your death. However, it will cost you a fortune to buy, and if you live for another twenty years, which you could easily do, your premiums will have more than covered the lump sum.

The answer is to buy an annuity at the same time. With an annuity you pay in a lump sum which will pay you a fixed income till you die.

So you use a lump sum to buy an annuity. The annuity then pays the premiums on the life insurance policy (and both run for as long as you do) and the life insurance policy pays the inheritance tax bill when it falls due.

The sweetener is that the annuity should also pay you around 5 per cent a year on top of the premiums in after-tax income. The drawback is that you need a lump sum to buy the annuity – it does mean that your heirs will receive less but that is more than made up for by the life policy coming in tax free.

GETTING HELP

Writing wills and inheritance tax planning are complicated issues – not least because the rules could change at any time. This is an area where you should get professional help if your affairs are in any way complicated.

A solicitor will help you with your will, a financial adviser or accountant with your inheritance tax planning. But close reading of this chapter will ensure that you understand the advice they are offering and are able to assess whether it is correct for you.

10 Insurance – You, Your Assets and Your Life

Household insurance · health insurance · life insurance

See also: Chapter 9, Wills and Inheritance Tax Planning

You could probably spend every penny that you earn on insurance premiums. There's your life, your health, long-term health care for your old age, medical, household, buildings, car, holiday, legal bills, pets, children, redundancy . . . right down to insuring your contact lenses and your golf clubs.

Or you could just insure what you have to – your car (it is a legal requirement) and your house (your mortgage lender will insist). But most of us veer towards a happy medium – and grudge every penny we spend on the rising insurance premiums. As you approach the major change in your life – giving up work – it is a good time to sit down and check that you have the correct policies, to cut down where you can and to make sure that you are getting the best value for money.

HOUSEHOLD INSURANCE

It would be a brave householder, in this day and age, who decided against insuring the contents and fabric of their home. None the less, with premiums rising by as much as 20 per cent a year, it is a tempting bill to cut.

So check that you are getting the best value for money. Subsidence has become an insurance bogey recently, after the series of recent dry summers. If your house is in an area where there is a lot of clay in the soil you may find your buildings insurance has rocketed, ahead of any likely claim. A different insurer may not take such a harsh line, so check around.

Household insurance premiums can be cut, without affecting the cover, if you agree to a larger excess on the policy (that means you pay the first tranche of any claim yourself). Or increase the security – you'll stop the burglars getting in, and hopefully qualify for a reduction on the policy.

Tip

Older people qualify for cheaper insurance with some companies and you can get a no-claims bonus. Age Concern have details.

Add-ons

Instead of taking out separate policies for some cover, you can add it on to your household policy. This can be cheaper, because most policies have a minimum charge. By adding on to your household insurance you'll avoid this and get the same cover for a few pounds a year. Things like bicycles, sports equipment, the food in your freezer, your caravan, vets' fees and legal bills can be covered in this way.

HEALTH INSURANCE

Up to now you've probably thought of health insurance in terms of membership of BUPA or PPP; you may have a critical illness plan; if you are self-employed you might have a permanent health insurance policy. Now you should also start thinking about a relatively new type of insurance – medical help for your old age.

Medical health insurance

Private medical insurance is not cheap. As an employee you may have been lucky enough to have the premiums paid by your employer as a perk of the job (though of course you will have to pay tax on the premiums). And no doubt you liked the idea of easy access to consultants and the privacy of a private room if you were an in-patient. Once you get older, you might want private medical insurance simply to jump any queues for operations. No one wants to wait for a year, in pain, for a hip operation.

But it doesn't come cheap. A married couple aged sixty to sixty-four will pay between £100 and £200 a month in premiums. Many insurance companies have special, cheaper, plans for older people. They tend to assume that you will be prepared to have the operation on the NHS if you don't have to wait longer than six weeks for it; they often cap the upper limit of what you can claim in a year; they may ask for an excess of say £100 on any claim. But this could reduce your premiums to £50–60 a month, if you go for the excess.

Once you reach sixty you can also qualify for tax relief on these premiums. Providing your scheme doesn't offer you a cash benefit for accepting an NHS bed then you can pay the premiums net of 25 per cent tax. If you're a 40 per cent payer, you claim the rest back using your tax form. But it is worthwhile checking what is on offer from the various companies and choosing the plan which suits you best. Don't just stick with the one your company opted for – what they wanted from a plan is undoubtedly different to what you will want once you retire.

Permanent health insurance

This is a misnamed form of insurance because it is really permanent ill-health insurance. It covers you for a lump sum or a monthly payment if you are off work for a substantial period through ill health or injury. How much you are paid and for how long depends on the policy you take out – the more money you get, the sooner it is paid and the longer it is paid for, the more expensive the premiums. Some employers provide this type of cover – if they don't, or you are self-employed, you can arrange it yourself.

Once you near retirement, this is an insurance policy you might allow to lapse. Your pension is not connected with your ability to work so you won't need insurance to make up any shortfall.

Critical illness insurance

Sometimes called dread disease cover, this insurance pays up if you get just that – the type of illness we all dread. Heart disease, cancer, a stroke, anything life-threatening that is included on the list of critical illnesses on the policy you take out. Aids is seldom on the list.

Started in South Africa, critical illness policies began to be written in this country in 1986 as an add-on to life insurance policies so that you got some money while you were still alive. Now they often stand as separate policies, and will pay up to £100,000 if an illness is diagnosed. But they are not cheap.

You'll need to undergo a medical for this cover, and of course any pre-existing conditions will be excluded.

Typically, a policy paying out £100,000 would cost a healthy fifty-five-year-old man £335 a month; a fifty-year-old woman £175 a month.

Old-age health care

As you get older, medical costs rise. You are more likely to be ill and more likely to need help in coping with it. A new type of insurance policy has come on to the market to help you out.

You can pay a lump sum or you can make monthly premiums. And in return the policy will cover you for nursing in your own home, help around the house or your stay in a nursing or residential home. And you can click into the policy at whichever level you need. If you start by getting help around the house, you can then move into residential accommodation later if you need it.

What you pay depends on your age when you take out the policy, your health, your sex and the level of benefit you want. Premiums and cover tend to be increased by the rate of inflation every year.

Examples

A fifty-five-year-old man wanting cover for £15,000 a year would pay around £90 a month.

A fifty-year-old woman would pay around £110 a month – because statistically they live a lot longer!

LIFE INSURANCE

This is one area where your financial criteria might well change as you get older. Life insurance is taken out for a variety of reasons – alongside your mortgage, as a savings plan, for inheritance tax planning. But in the main it is taken out to safeguard your dependants should anything happen to you.

A husband in his twenties or thirties with a wife at home and some children might buy it so that the family will have a lump sum to tide them over should he fall under the proverbial bus. Once that man reaches his mid-fifties, he may not feel the same need for the cover. The family are grown up, the mortgage may be paid, or very nearly, so there may be some capital in the bank and the pension cover may be sufficient for the needs of the financial dependants.

Alongside all this is the huge rise in the premiums for a life insurance policy taken out by an older person.

A healthy man wanting to cover a £100,000 lump sum to age sixty-five would pay:

Starting age	Monthly premium
20	£30.00
40	£50.00
60	£100.00

The reason is quite simply that the older you are, the more likely you are to die during the term of the policy. As a statistic the policy is weighted against you.

So think carefully about what you want from your policy before you decide to take on a new one. If you have a with-profits policy already running, keep it going if you can. Life insurance policies come into their own in the final years so try not to cash it in.

If you won't be able to afford the premiums once you retire there are four options open to you:

- cash it in
- take a loan against it
- make it paid up
- sell it to someone else.

Cashing it in

This is the worst option financially. You write to the insurance company and ask what the policy is worth. They will give you a figure and, if you accept it, you stop paying the premiums and get the lump sum they offer. Of course you lose the life cover.

A loan

Usually available up to about 80 per cent of the cash value; and although you pay interest on it you still get back the same pay-out.

Making the policy paid up

This means you can stop paying the premiums, but you wait until the end of the term before getting the money out. You won't get as much as you would have done if you'd continued to pay the premiums, but you'll get more than by cashing in the policy. The life cover will reduce to the paid-up value, but should go on earning bonuses with most companies.

Selling it to someone else

There are companies which specialize in buying and selling life insurance policies that are still running (the Association of Policy Marketmakers, address on page 163). They will sell your policy – either to individuals or to insurance companies. You get a lump sum – less commission – and it is usually up to a third more than you'd get from just cashing in the policy. You stop paying the premiums, and of course lose the life cover.

Terminally ill

Macabre point – if you've been diagnosed as terminally ill you may be able to cash your policy in immediately.

PART TWO

AT RETIREMENT

11 Investing at Retirement

Investing for capital growth · gilts · managed gilt fund · single premium bonds · deferred annuities

*See also: Chapter 2, Investing for Your Retirement;
Chapter 17, Investing after Retirement*

Once you retire, at whatever age, your investment criteria will change. You'll no longer want to invest in anything risky and you'll be twice as keen to make your money work for you.

The reason for this is quite simply that you have given up your job. Whatever you have now, plus your pension, has to last you to the end of your days. And, with luck, that could be quite far off yet.

At this stage, most people would quite like to put all their cash into a savings account where it would get interest added every year and there would be absolutely no chance of it going down the tubes.

However, nothing is that simple. The bogey which would thwart that plan is inflation. When it runs at a high level, perhaps into double figures, the value of your lump sum drops alarmingly. As your cost of living rises, your savings have to keep pace, or your lifestyle will slip. The value of your money needs to increase along with inflation, and the only way to do that is to go for capital growth rather than purely income from your lump sum. And when you go for capital growth you have to plug in to some sort of stock-market or property investment. And that means taking some risk. However you can limit the risk that you take.

The other problem you might have to face is low interest rates. If you are relying on interest from your savings and rates fall, your income will go down.

WHAT TO GIVE UP

Some investments carry more risk than others. At this stage in your financial life, when you've given up work, don't put your money into anything where there is a fair chance that you will lose it all.

Move away from the following:

Business expansion schemes. Although there are considerable tax advantages to this type of investment (see page 18), you can, and many people have, lost all of their investment. In most cases it is a five-year hold, which may not suit you anyway. But if you want to invest in a BES, stick to property and schemes with an assured exit, and invest through a good firm.

Penny shares. These are investments directly in shares which are very cheap. (In the old days it meant they cost less than a shilling a share.) The reason they cost so little is because the company is in a very precarious position. It will either recover, get taken over or go under. So you could make a bundle or lose your whole investment.

Shares. In general many people give up investing directly in shares because of the ups and downs of the stock market. They may need their money out during a bear market or just feel the risk is too high. For others, buying and selling shares becomes their hobby and they can do rather well out of it.

CAPITAL GROWTH OR INCOME?

With luck, your pension will support you financially at this stage in your life and you can use your savings for capital

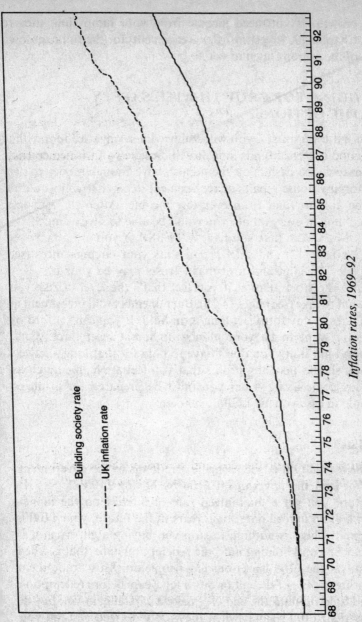

Inflation rates, 1969–92

Building society rate
UK inflation rate

68 69 70 71 72 73 74 75 76 77 78 79 80 81 82 83 84 85 86 87 88 89 90 91 92

growth. If you need income from your lump sum, turn to Chapter 17, Investing after Retirement, for the full run-down of the options open to you.

GOING FOR GROWTH WITH SAFETY – THE OPTIONS

First things first – you will still need a savings account with a good buffer of funds in it. It will provide you with emergency easy-access cash. You should also have enough money to pay for any house repairs or replacement items that you wouldn't be able to fund from everyday income. After all, with less coming in every month you won't be able to save as much.

Make sure that you have a TESSA if you are a taxpayer (see page 12) and a PEP if it suits your circumstances (see page 12). Unit and investment trusts may be your best way into the stock market if you feel that's the level of risk you want to take (see pages 14-15). But remember that investment in shares in any form is a long-term hold. If you can't afford or don't want to tie your money up for at least three years, don't put it in. You don't have to hold for that long – indeed you should take any profits that you feel are high enough as they come along – but you must be prepared for a longer hold in case you hit a falling market.

Gilts

What it is. Gilt-edged securities are loans to the government. You lend the government £100 by buying £100 of gilts. In return you get a guaranteed rate of interest on the money and, at an agreed date some years in the future, your £100 is repaid. There is nothing to stop you buying a gilt when it is launched and holding until the redemption date (that is when you get the £100 back) but few people do. Most trade them during the life of the gilt or buy a few years before redemption and hold on until the end. To make a capital gain you buy at less than £100 so that when they are redeemed at £100 you get the difference. For example, if you buy £100 of Treasury 8½ per cent, 2007 for £95 you will get 8½ per cent interest on £100 every year until 2007, when you will get £100 back for every £95 you paid. The rate of interest is fixed – those with a low rate of interest are usually cheaper, so you stand to make a larger capital gain on them if you hold on. Some are index-linked and so do better at times of high inflation. Gilts are always sold in £100 tranches.

Tip

If you buy gilts through the National Savings register you only pay a few pounds in charges so it is much cheaper than using a stockbroker, but you do risk your money being in the post for a day or two. If interest rates and therefore gilt prices move sharply you could get more, or less, for your money. Details of which gilts are on the register are available at large post offices.

Tax. You pay income tax, at your highest rate, on any interest you get. Interest is paid net if you buy through a stockbroker or financial intermediary, gross if you buy through the National Savings register. If you are a non-taxpayer and have had tax deducted, you can claim it back. No capital gains tax is charged on any profits you make from gilts.

Pros. Ideal for those wanting to try for a quick profit but prepared to hold until redemption if the price doesn't rise. And you know exactly how much you'll make as gilts are always redeemed at £100 (unless you still hold War Loan, or the like, which have no redemption date).

Cons. You won't make your fortune out of gilts – it is not a market to set the world on fire.

Managed gilt fund

What it is. It is a cross between an investment in gilts and a unit trust. You buy into the fund, which is a unit trust, and the managers invest your cash, and everybody else's, in gilts for you.

Tax. You pay income tax on any dividends you get in the normal way, and capital gains tax is charged on any profits you make over and above the CGT exemption limit.

Pros. You benefit from the expertise of the fund managers and you don't have to keep an eye on all the individual gilts yourself. Because your investments are spread over more gilts than you would be able to buy individually, you even out the peaks and troughs of winners and losers.

Cons. Charges on these funds, like unit trusts, can be high and you may be subject to CGT, which you don't pay from profits made directly from gilt dealing.

Single-premium bonds

What it is. As its name suggests, it is an investment of a single lump sum that is made to an insurance company. The cash is invested in a range of funds from shares to property, or it can be invested in with-profits funds – which is the safe option in retirement.

Tax. Income tax is paid within the bond and non-taxpayers cannot claim this back. There is no CGT liability but when the bond is cashed in, high-rate taxpayers have to pay tax at the higher rate on any profits that they have made. Investors can take up to 5 per cent of their investment out free of personal tax every year for twenty years. This 5 per cent is cumulative, so if you don't use it, you don't lose it.

Pros. One of the main advantages is the tax-free income that you can take every year. You can usually also switch money from fund to fund within the bond at no extra cost or for a reduced fee. If you are nearing sixty-five – and the additional age allowance tax relief (see page 126) – these bonds may keep your tax bill down.

Cons. It can be difficult to get your money back at short notice and the value of your investment does fluctuate, so there is a risk involved. There is usually a minimum sum that you have to cash in if you want to take part of your investment out. Charges are high – usually 5 per cent of your initial lump sum and an annual management charge of 1–1½ per cent; lower for larger sums. But they are lower than unit trust charges.

Tip
Watch out for brokers' single-premium bonds. The stock-broker or other financial adviser can add an additional ½–1 per cent on top of the usual charges.

Guaranteed income bond

What it is. A bond of from one to five years which is issued by insurance companies with a guaranteed net rate of interest. Buy from a reputable company.

Tax. Interest is paid net of basic tax and can't be reclaimed. Higher-rate payers can get the first 5 per cent of tax deferred to the end of the period.

Pros. Good to lock into high interest rates if rates are falling and rates are keener than you could get from a building society or bank.

Cons. Don't buy when interest rates are rising! Watch out when the bond matures – it could cost you your age allowance for that year.

12 Pensions and the Cash Sum

Drawing your pension · taking out an annuity · open-market option · different types of annuity · what to do with your lump sum

See also: Chapter 3, Pensions for the Employee; Chapter 4, Personal Pensions; Chapter 5, State Pensions and SERPs

Retirement has been called the first day of the rest of your life. Just before this happens, you will have to make some very important financial decisions which will decide just how well – and in what financial comfort – these years are spent.

STATE PENSION

You do not have a great deal of choice here. Retirement ages are fixed and a short time before you reach sixty (women) or sixty-five (men) the DSS will tell you what state pension you will get. But it is up to you to return the claim form, as the pension is not paid automatically. You can delay claiming your pension for up to five years and it will then be increased by $7\frac{1}{2}$ per cent for each year it is deferred.

PENSION FROM AN EMPLOYER

Final-salary scheme

Generally this is based on one sixtieth of final salary for every year with your present employer. Poorer schemes will pay less and public-sector pensions have an entirely different formula.

First of all your employer will tell you your 'final salary'. This could be the actual salary or a recent average, and if he is generous, could include bonuses, overtime and the taxable value of the company car. You will be quoted an annual pension amount, which cannot exceed two thirds of final salary.

Tip

An increasing number of company pension schemes are 'integrated' with the state pension – in other words your pension entitlement from the company will be reduced by the amount of state pension you can draw. So it is important to find out whether your scheme works on an integrated basis or not, as it will make a big difference to your total income.

The maximum you can take in cash is normally 1.5 times your final salary, though usually this is after forty years' service – though some schemes are more generous than others. However, big earners will find that if they joined a scheme in the last few years there will be a limit to the maximum sum. The pros and cons – mostly pros – of taking the lump sum are examined later in this chapter.

The other decisions an employee may have to make are:

Sorting out other deferred pensions. There may be pensions sitting with ex-employers, and although they should write to you before the normal retirement date of the scheme, trustees have been known to overlook deferred pensions.

AVCs. If they are in-house, they may add extra years on to your pension entitlement; otherwise there will be a cash sum to invest. You can take a tax-free lump sum from policies started up before April 1987, but after that date they must be used solely to provide a pension. The investment of funds from an AVC and a free-standing AVC are similar to personal pensions (see page 28).

Executive pensions. Generally the directors will be the trustees of these schemes, and will have a great deal of flexibility as to when and how they retire. But specialist advice will be needed.

Money-purchase schemes

Generally the fund built up at retirement is used to secure retirement benefits from the most competitive insurance company in the market-place. Normally the trustees can give some flexibility on the type of pension that can be secured, such as with or without pension increases. Benefits are subject to the same limits as final-salary schemes. A transfer to a personal pension plan, so that benefits can be taken on a phased basis, may be possible.

PENSIONS FOR THE SELF-EMPLOYED

Personal pensions have only been going since July 1988 so not that many people will be reaping the rewards in the near future.

Most self-employed people retiring in the nineties will have saved with the old-style Section 226 plan – often called a retirement annuity contract (RAC). But these are no longer available – although existing policies are still valid – and as time goes by, more and more personal pensions will come on stream. There are different rules for each type of policy.

Retirement annuity contracts

- You can normally only retire from age sixty onwards.
- There is no limit to the amount of pension you can buy.
- The maximum tax-free lump sum must not exceed three times your remaining pension. This will generally be a lot higher than a personal pension.
- To preserve maximum tax-free cash, you normally have to buy your pension annuity from the company where you have your RAC.

- If you have several RACs you can lump them together and go to the company which offers the best deal.

Personal pensions

- Retirement can be from age fifty onwards.
- There is no limit to the amount of pension you can buy.
- Generally the maximum tax-free cash is limited to 25 per cent of your fund.
- The 'contracted-out' element – the bit which equates to SERPs – is ignored from the lump-sum calculations.
- If you have different policies from different companies you can lump them altogether when you come to buy your pension.
- You can take your fund to the insurer paying the best rates. This 'open-market' option is looked at on page 100.

YOUR PENSION FUND

The words 'fund' and 'annuity' occur throughout this chapter. All types of investment-linked pension policies, whether they be RACs, personal pensions, company money-purchase schemes or AVCs, follow the same lines:

- They invest your cash to build up a fund of investments.
- When you retire this fund is converted into cash.
- The cash is used to buy an annuity.
- The income from the annuity is what provides your pension.

Investing your fund

- You want to make sure that the value of your fund is maximized and certain when retirement is on the horizon. This normally means converting your fund into cash-based investments at the highest rate of interest a few years before retirement date. You will then know exactly where you stand.

- You also want to make sure the annuity rate you get is the highest available at retirement. The return you get on this annuity is fixed for life and cannot be changed. The more you get, the more cash you will have in your pocket.

The open-market option

There is a very important concession which is ignored by far too many people:

- You normally have the right to take your personal pension fund to the insurance company which is offering the highest annuity rates.

This is called the 'open-market' option. Many people will not look beyond the existing insurer where they have been saving for a number of years, under the mistaken impression that their pension policy and the payment of the actual pension are irrevocably connected. This is not so. You can save with Company A but if Company B has the best annuity rates, take your fund to them.

This requires specialist advice and an intimate knowledge of the market-place. Annuity rates can be volatile and many insurance companies – perhaps the one where you have been saving – pay poor rates because they are not interested in this type of business.

Tip

The difference in the best rate and the worst on any given day can mean that you will get up to 25 per cent more in pension from one of the top companies – perhaps £10,000 a year, rather than £8,000 a year – so make sure you shop around.

The open-market option is not always available on RAC policies. It is possible to transfer your RAC into a personal pension to take advantage of better rates and earlier retirement. However, you may lose out on your lump sum, as this is generally higher with the old-style RACs than with a personal pension.

Different types of annuity

What is an annuity? It is basically a gamble by an insurance company on how long you are going to live. It is an agreement to pay you an income for life based on how long the insurer thinks that life will last.

This, unlike taking out life insurance, does not involve a medical examination. Insurance companies use actuaries who plough through piles of statistics on average life expectancy, and from these figures they work out the annuity rates. It is important to remember that your pension can die with you.

How much you get from your annuity depends on a number of factors:

Your sex. Women live longer than men so they will get less pension for their money, as the pension will normally be payable for a longer period. A man of sixty-five can expect to live until he is seventy-eight. A woman, on average, will make it to age eighty-two.

Your age. The older you are, the more you will get – after all, the odds move in favour of the insurance company that they will only pay out for a shorter period.

Interest rates. The higher rates are generally, the more you will receive.

Annuities come in a variety of shapes and sizes, and which type you choose depends on your particular set of circumstances. These are the principal types.

Level annuities. The income stays the same for the rest of your life.

Escalating annuities. The income rises by an agreed percentage every year – perhaps 3 or 5 per cent. This gives some protection against inflation but you get less for your money in the first few years to pay for this privilege.

With-profits annuities. Payments increase every year in line with bonuses, in much the same way as an endowment policy.

Unit-linked annuities. This means that your cash goes back into another insurance fund; how much you get depends on investment performance.

Index-linked annuities. Payments are linked to the rise in the Retail Prices Index.

The reason why there are so many different types has much to do with the old enemy, inflation. When you take a level annuity, your income stays the same for life. If inflation averages 5 per cent per annum, the buying power of this income will be halved in about fifteen years. If inflation hits 10 per cent, it will be halved in seven years.

The other annuities give you some protection against inflation – but at a price. You will get less income over the first few years but as you get older, so it will increase.

The following table shows how much a man of sixty-five can expect to get from a level annuity, one that escalates at 3 or 5 per cent, and another at the rate of inflation:

On a lump sum of £10,000

	Amount of pension (*per annum*)		
	Year 1	Year 5	Year 10
Level annuity	£1,200	£1,200	£1,200
Escalating at 3 per cent	£1,000	£1,159	£1,344
5 per cent	£850	£1,085	£1,385
Index linked (at 6.5 per cent p.a.)	£750	£1,028	£1,408

The good news is that in approximately five or ten years, the income from the inflation-beating annuities catches up with the level variety, and the longer you live, the more you are ahead of the game. So if longevity runs in your family, you may want to consider a with-profits or escalating contract. In the last few years, with-profits annuities have become very popular and have a generally good record of keeping their nose in front of inflation, although this is not guaranteed to happen for ever. Most people opt for the largest possible pension from the word go, and save any excess to help boost spending cash in later years.

Protecting your spouse

Most annuity quotations will initially be on your life only, and on death the pension dies with you. But if you want to protect your spouse, you should ask for the annuity to be on your joint lives. Then when one of you dies, the pension will continue to be paid to the survivor. The amount can be the same as before or a reduced amount of say 50 per cent. The last thing you want to do is to leave your spouse without any income.

Pension guarantee

Most annuities will now guarantee the pension for the first five years, even if you happened to die within that period. So if the worst did happen, your estate would still get paid for what remains of the five years.

Phased retirement

We mentioned on page 64 that having a personal pension plan divided into different segments was a good way of preparing for early retirement. But there is nothing to stop you from taking advantage of this at normal retirement age. In fact, the longer you can leave cashing in parts of your fund, the better the annuity rates will be, and you may find yourself in a lower tax bracket as well.

SHOULD YOU TAKE THE LUMP SUM?

You do not have to take your tax-free lump sum when you retire – but the vast majority of people do. And you do not have to take your maximum allowance. You can take a reduced amount and use the rest to get a higher pension.

Pros

- Cash gives you tremendous flexibility. You can go off on a world cruise, buy a new car and generally spend it on your personal enjoyment.
- Cash can be used to pay off the mortgage or other debts.
- Cash can be passed on to your family when you die. A pension dies with you – or when your spouse dies.
- Cash can be invested to produce both income and capital growth.
- Employees with reduced service – and therefore lower pension – can use the cash to buy a 'purchased' annuity. This gets better tax treatment than the 'compulsory' annuity which you are obliged to buy with your pension fund, and can be a good way of increasing your income.
- The higher your tax rate, the better it is to take the money. Your pension will be taxed at the top rate but a lower pension may bring you back to the standard rate. At the same time, cash can be invested in tax-free investments such as National Savings certificates and PEPs.
- You can give the cash to your spouse to invest. This idea may fill you with horror, but it can be very tax-efficient. Both husband and wife have their own tax allowances and if a wife has little or no income, the earnings on the investments – as well as any capital gains – can be largely tax-free.
- If you are in poor health, the advantages of taking the cash are obvious, bearing in mind that a pension can die with you.
- If you are in very poor health the taxman may let you take the full pension fund in cash.

Cons

- The major disadvantage in taking the money is that your pension will be reduced. If income is important you may consider going for a higher pension instead. You need to sit down and work out a careful budget just before you retire.

- If you are an employee and your pension fund has an excellent record of paying top-whack pension increases, you will be forfeiting these by having a lower pension.

13 Your Home

Staying put · sheltered housing · pay off your mortgage? · negative equity

See also: Chapter 18, Making Ends Meet

Standing on the threshold of retirement is a good time to take a long hard look at your home. Is it the right one for you now and will it meet your needs for the future? It may have been in the right catchment area for schools when the children were young, or in the city centre to keep commuting times down, or on a bus route for work, or perhaps it has a big garden because you liked having plenty of space. But your priorities are changing. You don't have to live in any relationship to the place where you used to work; a big garden can be a real handicap as you get older, culminating in having to pay a gardener to do the lawn-mowing and weeding. You may now prefer to have easy access to the shops or you may want to move to a village, or the coast, or near to your children. It is worthwhile sitting down and working out just what you want from your home, and what you will want from it in the years to come. Old people and new draughts don't go together, so they say, so if you feel you must move, now might be the time to do it.

Maintenance

As you worked your way up the career ladder, and perhaps had a growing family, your house too will have expanded. The chances are that you reach retirement living in the largest home you've had. And the bigger the house the more it costs to maintain it. From the roof to the foundations, it will cost you plenty if anything goes wrong. So, before you take any decisions on whether or not to move, it could be very worthwhile getting a survey done on your own house.

This will show up anything that is likely to go wrong in the coming years. If you know that the roof will need replacing or there's a problem with the drains, you can write these costs into your equation, and it will also alert you to anything that a potential buyer will find out and be discouraged by.

PROS AND CONS OF MOVING

Moving house is a very expensive exercise. Regardless of whether you are buying something larger or smaller the sheer cost of selling one house, buying another and getting your furniture shifted is staggering. On top of that there's the stress factor.

On the other hand, you may be taking some capital out if you're buying a smaller place. And if you shift down a council tax band or two, there'll be a saving there too.

SHELTERED ACCOMMODATION

At the moment you are probably much too young and able even to consider sheltered housing. But it is worth knowing what is on offer and how the system works – even if it is just so that you can let your parents know.

Sheltered accommodation usually consists of a group of self-contained flats or bungalows, normally with a live-in warden, alarm system and communal areas such as lounges and laundry.

There is normally an age restriction – usually around fifty-five. You have to be over that age to buy and, of course, the people you sell to must also be over that age. So it restricts the market you can sell into.

How to buy

Outright. You pay the full price for the property.

Mortgage. If you need a mortgage a building society or bank will be happy to give you one so long as you can prove an ability to repay. So if your pension is big enough you can take out a home loan – though it might be over ten years instead of the more usual twenty-five. Or you could go for an interest-only loan, with the capital being repaid when the property is sold.

Shared ownership. Some councils and housing associations allow you to buy through this scheme. You buy a percentage of the property and pay rent on the rest. When the property is sold, you get the same percentage of the price back.

Buying at a discount. Some developers of sheltered housing will sell to you at a discount – say 80 per cent of the full price. When you sell, you get 80 per cent of the price back.

THE MORTGAGE

For many people, paying off the mortgage becomes a priority at retirement. Starting out on the next stage of their life, on a reduced income, they like to feel that the monthly burden of debt is off their shoulders and the house is theirs.

Psychologically, it can be a wonderful feeling to know that the slate is clean and the mortgage paid off. But is it a good idea?

To pay or not to pay it off

Whether or not you pay off your mortgage on retirement depends on a number of factors:

- whether you can afford the monthly repayments
- how much capital you have

- if you have a repayment mortgage
- if you have an endowment mortgage.

Monthly repayments

If you can afford the repayments from your pension there is nothing at all to stop you just keeping on paying the mortgage. Your mortgage lender will not be in the least concerned that you are paying out of your pension instead of your salary as long as you don't miss any payments. However, if you cannot afford the payments out of your monthly income and you have enough capital to pay off the mortgage, then read on.

Capital

If you have enough cash to pay off your mortgage easily, then it becomes an option for you. The chances are that the interest you are paying on your loan – less tax relief at 25 per cent on the first £30,000 of your mortgage (20 per cent from April 1994) – is more than the interest you get on your savings. So it will be costing you money to service this loan.

But don't run yourself short to pay off the mortgage. Because of the tax relief you get, a home loan is the cheapest form of borrowing there is. Don't borrow elsewhere to pay off the mortgage and don't pay it off if it means you will have to take out a loan for, say, a car or a holiday.

Repayment mortgage

A repayment mortgage is the type where you make one payment each month to the mortgage lender; part of the money pays interest on the loan and part refunds some of the capital of the mortgage. As a rule of thumb, if you are within four years of the end of a loan of over twenty years, and you can easily afford it, pay off your mortgage.

Endowment mortgage

An endowment mortgage is the type where you make two monthly payments. One is the interest on the loan to the lender and the other is an insurance premium on an endowment policy. At the end of the term – usually twenty-five years – the endowment policy should be large enough to pay off the loan and leave you with a lump sum. The money accumulating in the endowment policy gets larger as the years go on because you are paying in cash every month, and the money already in the fund is making more money through investment. As such it is much better to let this policy run – it really comes into its own in the last few years.

On top of that, endowment policies are also life insurance policies. If the policyholder dies, the policy pays off the mortgage automatically, and that's another plus factor for keeping it going. If you really can't afford the premiums, but could manage to keep paying the interest to the mortgage lender, you'd be better to make the policy 'paid up', rather than cashing it in. See page 84.

NEGATIVE EQUITY

In 1992, the financial buzzword was 'negative equity'. What it means is that your home has become worth less than your mortgage. If you paid £130,000 for your house, taking a mortgage of £120,000, and now find that the value of your property has fallen to £100,000, what you have is £20,000 of negative equity in your house.

One answer on offer by some building societies is for you to take out an unsecured loan for the negative equity. So, in the above example, you would sell your home for £100,000, take out an unsecured loan for £20,000 and so pay off the mortgage. It leaves you, however, with a £20,000 debt. The rate of interest on the unsecured loan is a lot higher than the mortgage rate, for three reasons:

- there is no tax relief
- the loan is unsecured and therefore riskier to the lender
- you usually have to pay it back over a shorter term.

So don't be tempted down this route unless you have given the whole issue a lot of thought.

It may be in your interest just to sit tight and wait until house prices rise again.

Or you can move your loan when you move house, substituting the new home for the old one as security. The Inland Revenue no longer insist that you forfeit tax relief as a result.

14 Getting Help

DSS benefits – Unemployment Benefit · Income Support · Housing Benefit · Council-tax Benefit · Social Fund · charities – dealing with debt

See also: Chapter 18, Making Ends Meet

Not everyone giving up work is stepping into retirement with a large lump sum and a monthly pension to look forward to spending.

For many, the golden years will be tarnished with the thought that they really are not going to be able to manage financially.

Well, help is available – from the DSS and from thousands of charities around the country.

DSS BENEFITS

No one should ever feel too 'proud' to accept money from the Department of Social Security. The benefits they pay out are funded by National Insurance contributions – which you have paid into throughout your working life. So all you are doing is claiming from a 'policy' which you have been contributing to for years.

All pensioners automatically get free prescriptions – and you claim simply by ticking the correct box on the back of the prescription and signing it.

> **Tip**
> If you're not sure whether or not you can claim for something, ask for help from the DSS itself. That doesn't necessarily mean a trip to the local office. Ring them on a freephone number – 0800 666555. They can't answer specific inquiries, but they can tell you what you need to know about general points.

Unemployment benefit

What it is. A fortnightly payment for those out of work and actively seeking another job. It is dependent on your National Insurance contributions, and it can be paid for a maximum of a year.

Tax. This benefit is taxable if your annual income exceeds your tax-free allowances.

What you get. The current rate is £44.65 for women under sixty or men under sixty-five. Over that age the benefit will be based on personal retirement pension entitlements. There is an extra £33.70 a week if you have a dependent wife or husband, and that increases to £45.15 if you are a woman over sixty or a man over sixty-five. Once men reach seventy and women sixty-five they are not entitled to Unemployment Benefit, and you cannot claim it if you are getting paid your state retirement pension.

How to claim. Sign on at your local unemployment office. You'll need your National Insurance number and your P45.

Income support

What it is. This is a benefit for people who cannot manage on the money they have. In order to qualify, your savings must be below £8,000 – and if your savings are between £3,000 and £8,000, you will lose part of your benefit.

Tax. This benefit is taxable if your annual income exceeds your tax-free allowances.

What you get. Income Support depends on several factors – your age, your weekly income, your savings and your dependants – but if you qualify you also get other financial help. These are free NHS eye tests and vouchers for glasses, dental treatment, wigs and fabric supports, and travelling costs to and from hospital. You may also qualify for help with the Council-tax and Housing Benefit, and with your mortgage interest.

Tip

If your savings are just over £8,000 it might be worthwhile using some of the money to pay off any loans you have, such as the mortgage or car loan. Even if you don't qualify for much Income Support, the very fact that you qualify at all allows you plenty of other extras.

How to claim. Ask the DSS for a claim form.

Housing Benefit

What it is. This is a payment to help you to pay your rent. If you are a council tenant your rent will be reduced; otherwise it will be paid to you or direct to your landlord. You won't qualify if your savings top £16,000 and you'll get less benefit if you have any savings over £3,000.

Tax. This benefit is tax free.

What you get. Housing Benefit is means-tested and depends on how much money you have coming in each week, the size of your family, your savings and how much your rent is.

How to claim. If you are on Income Support you will automatically get a Housing Benefit claim form with your first claim for Income Support; otherwise you can get one at your council offices or from the DSS or your local CAB.

Council-tax Benefit

What it is. This is a benefit which helps people who cannot afford the council tax. Unlike the community charge, there is no minimum that you have to find yourself: you can qualify to have the whole tax paid. But there is no help with water rates.

If you live alone, your bill will be reduced by 25 per cent as a single-person concession.

Tax. This benefit is tax free.

What you get. How much help you get depends on your income, savings, the size of your family and whether you have a disability.

How to claim. Contact your local council office.

Social Fund

What it is. It is a series of funds which help you to buy things such as a washing-machine or bed that you couldn't afford out of normal income. If you are over sixty you must have savings of less than £1,000 (£500 if you are under sixty) to qualify.

Tax. This benefit is tax free.

What you get. That depends on how much money is left in the Social Fund of your particular area. You might get the full amount or you might get nothing at all.

How to claim. Contact your local DSS office.

The Social Fund covers Budget Loans, Crisis Loans, and Community Care Grants.

- Crisis Loans – available to everyone on application for help during a crisis.
- Budget Loans – available to people who have been on Income Support for twenty-six weeks; the loans must be repaid from your weekly Income Support payments.

- Community Care Grants – available only to certain categories of people, for example ex-prisoners.

Other DSS benefits

You may also qualify for help with funeral expenses (savings below £1,000) and fuel bills in very cold weather, the Disabled Living Allowance, the Attendance Allowance, Invalidity Pension and Invalidity Allowance. Contact the DSS, your local CAB or Advice Shop for further details on all these benefits.

Tip
You don't have to be completely blind to be registered as a blind person, and this entitles you to more help which makes the business of living easier.

There is also one other payment the DSS makes – and you get it regardless of how well off you are. This is the Christmas bonus. When you collect your pension at the beginning of December you will get an extra £10 to help you with your Christmas expenses. Don't spend it all in one shop!

CHARITIES

There are about 1,700 charities in this country, paying out almost £90 million every year. So if you are really stuck, it is worth giving them a call or writing to them.

They range from service and ex-service charities, and those supporting particular occupations or trades, to charities for specific illnesses or disabilities or local to a particular area.

There is a useful book detailing all the charities, saying who is eligible and giving the relevant address. This is the *Guide to Grants for Individuals in Need*; it should be available in CABs, DSS offices and some large libraries. You can buy it yourself (from the address given in Appendix 2), but it is expensive.

DEBT

You may start out by getting credit – but if you can't make the payments it soon turns into debt. Once you start down the slippery slope and ignore the warnings, it is very difficult to face the problem alone. Particularly if you are older, because you may feel there is a stigma attached to not being able to handle your financial affairs. Younger people find it easier to get help because they don't feel this stigma so acutely. Take a leaf out of their book.

No one sets out deliberately to get into debt. And it is seldom overspending which causes it – it is more likely to be a crisis such as death, divorce, serious illness or job loss. Or quite simply not having enough money to live on. Once you are in debt the problem compounds itself because you find yourself paying high rates of interest on the money you owe, and on the arrears, and once this starts to snowball you're sunk. If you can't pay the interest every month you will never be able to pay off the capital. So you must get help.

Professional debt counsellors are your answer. Try your local council to see if they have a money advice centre; or your nearest Citizens Advice Bureau. There's a tried and tested path for helping people like you – and it does work. It doesn't happen overnight, and it is not necessarily quick and easy, but it will get you out of debt. And that is a promise. But you must take that first step yourself, and go and get help.

15 Expatriate Pensions

What happens to your tax and your state and company pension if you want to retire abroad

See also: Chapter 2, Investing for Your Retirement; Chapter 8, Early Retirement

There are many reasons why you may want to retire abroad. It could be the need of a warmer climate or simply a better standard of living – all that cheap wine and cigarettes! On the other hand, you may be avoiding capital gains tax on the sale of your business or have a holiday home where you would prefer to live in retirement.

But whatever the reasons, there will be a variety of hurdles to overcome before you can truly say you have severed all the ties with the old country and settled into the new one. Apart from all the problems in buying an overseas property and finding out about health care, there will also be a number of important financial questions to be answered.

Non-residency

The UK taxman will need a lot of convincing if you are going to escape from his clutches. You will need to prove you have severed all connections – such as selling your UK house, buying another abroad and obtaining some form of official registration in your new country; *then* he will quickly grant 'conditional non-resident' status. But it will generally be another three years before this becomes final. The taxman wants to ensure you are not taking an extended holiday just to avoid paying him!

Visits to the UK

To remain a non-resident, the rules about coming back to the UK are quite strict:

- You cannot spend more than 183 days in the UK in any one tax year.
- You cannot spend more than ninety days on average in the UK over four consecutive tax years.
- Following the 1993 Budget change, you can now have 'available accommodation' in the UK.

Inflation

This problem is not just limited to the UK, it is worldwide. Currently it is under control here, but take care you do not jump from the frying-pan into the fire. Many expats left the UK in the seventies and eighties to live in Spain because of the high cost of living here. But today prices are rising at a far higher rate in Spain than they are in Britain. In fact many Brits who went to live there in the seventies and eighties when Spain was a 'cheap' country, now find it is as expensive as, or even more expensive than, Britain.

Currency

If your income is in pounds, you will have to convert at least part of it into local currency for day-to-day living expenses. And now you must play on the swings and roundabouts of the currency game. Stable currencies are a great comfort to the expat who is able to budget accordingly. But as we saw when the UK left the Exchange Rate Mechanism in 1992, the value of the pound can suddenly plummet. Brits living in France saw the value of their pensions drop by more than 10 per cent overnight. And if you have a loan in a foreign currency, you could suddenly find you owe more than you did at the outset.

Exchange control

Britain has no exchange controls and money can move freely in and out. But it is not so in some other countries, which may impose controls and restrict you from taking money out of the country.

> **Tip**
> If you take a lump sum from your pension plan, it is generally better to invest it 'offshore' – in a safe and efficient tax haven such as the Channel Islands or the Isle of Man – rather than risk extra taxes or exchange controls in your new country.

TAXATION

Although you have escaped abroad, it is quite likely that most, or even all, of your income actually originates in the UK. This will probably be your pension, dividends on shares or interest from a bank or building society. As a general rule, income which arises in the UK has to be taxed in the UK.

However, to the rescue comes the very important double-taxation agreement. This stops income being taxed twice, both here and in your new country. Britain has an agreement with over seventy different countries, including all the most popular retirement areas. Normally, you will be exempt in the UK for all or most of the tax, and pay it in your new country.

> **Tip**
> Tax rates in some countries are a lot higher than in the UK, so it may be cheaper for you to have the income taxed here rather than abroad. Check this carefully before acting. It is also possible to claim your UK personal tax allowance on income arising in the UK, such as interest and pensions, even after you have left the country.

Different taxes

You may think the Inland Revenue has enough rules and regulations to last a lifetime. But beware many foreign states go in for a whole range of taxes which are totally alien to the UK. Some countries have an annual wealth tax as well as extra property taxes. In addition, some impose taxes on foreign residents and charge death duties between husband and wife.

Capital gains tax

This will generally not affect most expats who sell their main residence in the UK and emigrate. But if you have a second property or a business to sell, you will have to pay capital gains tax on your profits at your top rate of tax if you are a UK resident subject to retirement relief (see page 129).

For this reason, it is better to wait until you are a non-resident before realizing any gains. Timing is important and advice essential. But remember that it is the date of contract which is normally taken into account, not the date when you get the money.

Inheritance tax

Although you may live abroad, the taxman could still want a share of your estate on death. If this is going to be a problem, you have to convince the Inland Revenue that you are *domiciled* abroad. This is different from nationality or residence, in that your domicile is where you have your permanent home.

Bank and building society interest

If you can now certify that you are non-resident, the interest will be paid without deduction of tax. Many institutions have offshore accounts for expats where the interest is automatically paid gross.

Dividends

These were generally paid with a tax credit showing that 25 per cent tax has already been deducted. If you are in a country where there is a double-taxation agreement, you can get a refund of part of this deduction – normally 15 per cent – but from 6 April 1993 the tax credit was reduced to 20 per cent.

PAYMENT OF PENSIONS

State pensions

There will be no problem in getting your pension paid abroad, either into a local bank or by cheque. It is normally subject to UK tax, but if it is your only income here, it will generally be paid gross. However, if you have another pension, it will be added to the overall total, and tax charged on both of them.

If your new country has a double-taxation agreement with the UK, it can be taxed there rather than in Britain – but make sure tax rates are not higher in your new country.

State pensions are reviewed every year, and normally rise in line with inflation. Expats will only receive these increases if the UK has a reciprocal agreement with the country concerned. Common-market countries, most other European countries and the USA are covered. However, many areas, such as Australia, Canada and New Zealand do not participate, and you will probably find that the pension is frozen at the rate which applied when you went overseas.

Company pensions

These can be paid worldwide, but generally after deduction of tax. Once again, if there is a double-taxation agreement, the pension can be taxed abroad.

Personal pensions

Your pension derives from the annuity which you buy on retirement. Annuities can be paid with tax already deducted, in the same way as company pensions. You should ask the insurance company to apply to the Inland Revenue for a suitable authorization.

Tip

If you are using other money to buy an annuity – perhaps your tax-free lump sum – consider buying an annuity with an offshore life company. The income would automatically be paid gross.

---

16 You and Your Tax

Income tax · age allowance · capital gains tax · retirement relief

See also: Chapter 9, Wills and Inheritance Tax Planning

Mistakenly, many people think that once they retire they don't have to pay tax any more. Wrong. We all have to pay our due to the Inland Revenue, no matter how old or how young we are, if our annual income exceeds our annual allowances. It is as simple as that.

However, as you get older your allowances go up so you do get a bit of help from the taxman. And there are plenty of simple steps you can take to keep your tax bill to a minimum.

INCOME TAX

Income tax is the slice of money that the Inland Revenue takes out of your annual income if it is greater than your personal allowances. We all have a personal allowance – of £3,445 in the 1993–4 tax year. If you are married there will be a married couple's allowance – £1,720 for 1993–4 – on top of that. It is automatically paid to the husband, but the wife can claim her share, or more.

Married couple's allowance

A wife wanting half the allowance can get it simply by writing to her tax office and asking for it. She does not need the permission of her husband, though he will be told about it because his tax bill will increase when she is allotted half the married couple's allowance. If the wife wants more than half of the allowance she needs to apply jointly with her husband. And the claims must be made before the start of the tax year.

If a wife has a higher tax rate than her husband, or she is a taxpayer and he is not, perhaps because she is still working after he has retired, then it would be in their interest for her to make this claim. From 6 April 1994, this will not work. The tax relief on a married couple's allowances is being reduced to 20 per cent for everyone.

Personal allowance

The personal allowance cannot be transferred from one spouse to the other.

But a couple should make very sure that they are using both personal allowances to the full. In some families, if the wife does not work, she may not be offsetting her personal allowance, while the husband has most of the savings in his name. By transferring them to his wife, who could then claim the interest on the savings gross, they will get a much higher rate of interest.

Example

John Brown is a taxpayer at 25 per cent, his wife Beth pays no tax. They have savings of £10,000 getting 10 per cent interest.

Invested in John's name the interest paid is £750 a year
Invested in Beth's name the interest paid is £1,000 a year
because she does not have tax at 25 per cent deducted.

If one partner is a higher-rate taxpayer and the other an ordinary-rate payer, again there is a saving to be made by transferring any money to the account of the lower payer.

> **Tip**
> If you have a joint account, the Inland Revenue will automatically deem you to be receiving half the interest each. You can elect to have one partner receive all the interest but still keep the capital in joint names.

AGE ALLOWANCE

Once you reach the age of sixty-five your personal and married couple's allowances go up. And the new allowances apply in the tax year of your sixty-fifth birthday. The higher married couple's allowance is effective as soon as one partner reaches the age of sixty-five, regardless of the age of the other.

The allowances go up again at age seventy-five.

In the 1993–4 tax year the allowances are:

- personal allowance, age 65–74 . . . £4,200
- married couple's allowance, age 65–74 . . . £2,465
- personal allowance, age 75 and over . . . £4,370
- married couple's allowance, age 75 and over . . . £2,505

In 1994–5, the tax relief on the married couple's allowance is being reduced to 20 per cent. To compensate, the band will be widened by £200:

65–74 . . . £2,665
75 and over . . . £2,705

The reason the age allowances are given is to help older people by giving them an extra tax break. However, if you are rich enough not to need the help, then the Inland Revenue takes it back again.

'Rich enough', in Inland Revenue terms, means having an annual income of over £14,200 in the 1993–4 tax year. The way the system works is that you get the allowance you are entitled to, and if your income exceeds the top barrier then the Revenue claws it back again. You lose £1 in tax for every

£2 you are over until you get back to the ordinary personal allowance again. That clawback means you are paying tax at what seems swingeing rates, so if you are on the borderline, it is worth doing some tax planning.

Avoid the clawback

What you need is to reduce your income. And you can do it by:

- moving into tax-free or tax-deferred investments
- going for a capital gain instead.

Tax-free investments

The simplest and safest move is to put some of your savings into National Savings certificates. The interest is added tax-free to your lump sum, and provided that you hold for the five years, the rate of interest is quite acceptable. The first tranche of interest on the National Savings ordinary account is also tax-free so you could lodge some cash there too.

Tip

If you feel like a little bit of a gamble with your money put £1,000 or so into Premium Bonds – no interest is paid but you do have a 15,000:1 chance of a win. You pay no tax on any winnings and there is no guarantee that you will ever get more than your initial investment back – but, remember, someone wins the jackpot every month and at least you do get your money back.

Capital gain

Switching some of your money into gilts might be a sensible move (see page 92). Use a low-interest short gilt – that means it will be redeemed in a few years' time – because you don't want to tie up your money for too long. Or you could invest in what are known as zero-dividend preference shares on investment trusts. You get no income from them, but a predictable capital gain.

Or switch into a with-profit bond (see page 17) where your money should make an investment return, but you can also take 5 per cent a year out as income, tax-free to you. And the 5 per cent you take will not affect your age allowance.

CAPITAL GAINS TAX

If you make a capital gain on anything, such as shares, you will have to pay capital gains tax. The first tranche of profit is CGT-free – £5,800 in the 1993–4 tax year; thereafter you pay the tax at your top rate. If you are not a taxpayer and have a CGT liability, you will pay at 20 per cent on the first £2,000 taxable gains.

Indexation

The Inland Revenue does accept that inflationary gains are not real gains so they allow you to add inflation into your sums before declaring your CGT profit. You do this by 'indexing' your gains. Indexation allowance tables are published regularly by the Inland Revenue and it is possible to do the sums yourself, but if you reach this stage in your financial affairs, it might be wise to get some professional advice.

If you are selling something you bought before 31 March 1982 you can discount any profit you made before that date. That effectively writes off the inflationary years of the 1970s. You just use the market value of the item on 31 March 1982 and index the profits you have made since.

CGT-free

If you hold gilts for at least a year, any gain you make is free of capital gains tax.

If you are selling assets such as paintings or antiques, you can take the first £6,000 profit CGT-free, though the rules are more complicated for sets of things, such as chairs. There are other categories of items which are free of CGT, such as classic cars, profits from selling a Victoria Cross or George Cross medal that you have won, the proceeds from a life insurance policy (unless bought second-hand), anything that's not expected to last more than fifty years – such as a racehorse – and timber, providing you're not in the lumber business.

RETIREMENT RELIEF

If you're retiring due to ill health or are over fifty-five, you get some tax relief on the money you make from selling your business.

To qualify you must be:

- selling the whole or part of your business which you have owned for over a year
- selling shares in a business in which you were a full-time director and in which you and your family have a large percentage of the voting rights.

What you get

If you have owned the business for at least ten years you get:

- the first £150,000 of capital gains completely CGT-free
- half the gain between £150,000 and £600,000 is CGT-free.

If you owned the business for less than ten years you get 10 per cent of the maximum relief for every complete year of ownership. So if you owned it for seven and a half years, you would get 70 per cent of the relief.

Entrepreneurs reinvesting in a new business the proceeds of selling the old one can put off paying the capital gains tax.

Again, this is specialist tax planning and although it is worth knowing in general terms what you are likely to be entitled to, it is worth getting professional help to ensure that you take advantage of all the tax reliefs you are entitled to.

PART THREE

AFTER RETIREMENT

17 Investing after Retirement

Tax · investing for income · annuities · taking a job

See also: Chapter 2, Investing for Your Retirement;
Chapter 11, Investing at Retirement

Now that you've been retired a while, it is time to take a
fresh look at your finances.

In your fifties, you were prepared to risk a little of your
capital to try to make a quick gain.

In your sixties, you preferred less risk but were still pushing
your capital to make it grow in real terms.

In your seventies, it is time to take stock again. By this
stage you might find you don't want to take any more risks
at all. Income may be what you want, or need. Or it may just
be that you've grown past wanting to risk any of your money
at all. And there's nothing wrong with that.

What you have now, plus your pensions, has to see you
through to the end. You're now past the time biblically
allotted, of three score years and ten – though hopefully you
have plenty of full years ahead of you. None the less, you
may not want to see your nest-egg take a dive in the stock
market because economic events have turned against you.
It's security-first time.

TAX

You may now qualify for the age allowance (see page 126) so
keep a careful check to ensure that your income is not
drifting over the upper limit. If it is, and you can't shuffle

your funds to avoid moving out of the age-allowance claw-back band you might start to think about giving some of your capital away.

Quite simply you can give up to £3,000 a year away without paying any inheritance tax on it, and if you need to do more than that, turn back to Chapter 9 for further advice.

But remember, don't give away too much and leave yourself short in later years when you might need the cash for medical or nursing care or to pay for a gardener or window-cleaner.

Non-taxpayers

You might find that, as you get older and your tax-free allowances rise, you become a non-taxpayer. Check your figures carefully and if that is indeed the case then you should ensure that any interest you get on your savings is paid gross – that is before tax is deducted. Otherwise you will have to claim it back.

Non-taxpayers should fill in form R85 at their local bank or building society and the tax will automatically be paid gross. If during the year they find that they should after all be paying tax on the interest, they must write immediately to the Inland Revenue – that way they will avoid being fined.

INCOME OPTIONS

If you are looking for straight, no-risk income then you are looking at bank and building society and National Savings accounts. Your money is safe there – and the interest is added regularly.

For the record, here are the compensation schemes, but if you put your money with a well-known bank or building society in this country it is not likely that you will ever have to make use of them:

Building societies. You get back 90 per cent of the first £20,000 of savings; if husband and wife have a joint account, you get 90 per cent of the first £40,000.

Banks. You get 75 per cent of the first £20,000; with joint accounts you get 75 per cent of the first £40,000.

National Savings accounts. These are backed by the government, so no compensation scheme is needed. You will always get your money back.

Bank or building-society savings account

What it is. A savings account that pays interest regularly – either annually, six-monthly, quarterly or monthly. The more money you have in the account, and the longer you are prepared to tie it up, the higher the rate of interest you will get.

Tax. These accounts have basic-rate tax automatically deducted from the interest, so if you pay at a lower rate tell the Inland Revenue; if you are a non-taxpayer, sign the appropriate form. Higher-rate taxpayers declare the interest on their tax form and will have to pay up.

How much. There is usually a minimum investment on these accounts of £1 – but for those paying higher rates of interest the minimum can be much higher. There is seldom a maximum.

Tip
Watch out for what is known as past issues. These are bank or building society accounts that are now obsolete because a new better account has been brought in. Your money won't automatically be transferred into the better account, so check the adverts and leaflets on the counter when you are next paying in or withdrawing money.

National Savings

Investment account

What it is. A savings account paying a known rate of interest.

Tax. The interest is added gross but taxpayers will have to pay up.

How much. Minimum of £5 and maximum of £100,000.

Watch out. You need to give a month's notice of any withdrawals.

Ordinary account

What it is. A savings account that pays more interest if you have over £500 in the account.

Tax. The first £70 of interest is tax-free (£140 for husband and wife) so it can be ideal for those on the age allowance threshold. Thereafter it is taxable but paid gross.

How much. Minimum is £5; maximum is £10,000.

Watch out. Interest is added from the month following the one in which you make the deposit, and is stopped the month before the one in which you withdraw. So pay in on the last day of a month and withdraw on the first day to get maximum interest on your money.

Income bonds

What it is. An account which pays income monthly and so can be ideal for those who need to use their capital to supplement their day-to-day living expenses.

Tax. Interest is paid gross, but is subject to tax if you are a taxpayer.

How much. Minimum of £2,000 and maximum of £250,000.

Watch out. Three months' notice to cash in income bonds – which you must buy and sell in £1,000 tranches. You won't get your first monthly payment until the bonds have been invested for six weeks and if you cash in a bond within twelve months of buying it, you only get half the normal rate of interest.

Capital bonds

What it is. A five-year hold gives you a lump sum. You can get your money out earlier, but the rate of interest rises the longer you hold, so don't invest if you don't think you can hold for the full five years.

Tax. Interest is taxable but you don't get it until the end of the five years. However, if you are a taxpayer, you'll have to pay the tax on the interest every year, so you'll be in the unusual position of paying tax on interest you haven't received.

How much. Minimum £100 and maximum £250,000.

Watch out. The rate of interest is fixed for the term so only buy at times when rates are high.

Children's bonds

What it is. This is not something you can buy for yourself, but you might like to invest for grandchildren or godchildren who are under the age of sixteen. Parents hold the bonds until the child is sixteen, and then the child is responsible for the bond. It is a five-year hold with an annual rate of interest and a bonus added at the end. The rate is fixed at the outset but varies as various series are withdrawn and new ones launched. Buy when rates are high.

Tax. Interest is tax free.

How much. Minimum £25, maximum £1,000.

Watch out. Children can only have £1,000 in the bond so don't overbuy.

FIRST option bond

What it is. A one-year bond with the rate of interest fixed and guaranteed when you buy.

Tax. Basic-rate tax is deducted from the interest.

How much. Minimum £1,000 and maximum of £250,000.

Watch out. You lose a lot of interest if you don't hold for the full year. National Savings will write two weeks before the bond is due to mature and you only have two weeks to withdraw it; otherwise you lock in for another twelve months. This bond is, at times, withdrawn altogether.

> **Tip**
> If interest rates are on the way down, fixed-interest National Savings products are often withdrawn on the evening of an interest-rate change. If you want to lock in, move fast on any rate-change announcements.

Savings certificates

What it is. A five-year hold offering a fixed rate of interest guaranteed but sliding. You get a lot more interest if you hold for the full five years.

Tax. Savings certificates pay interest tax-free.

How much. Varies, but usually a minimum of £100 to maximum of £10,000. You can often add extra above that limit if you are reinvesting from other savings certificates.

Watch out. Poor rate of interest if you cash in early and once the five-year term is up.

Index-linked savings certificates

What it is. Similar to the basic certificates except that the rate of interest is linked to inflation. Usually you get the annual rate of inflation as your rate of interest, and a bonus added at the end of five years.

Tax. Tax-free.

How much. Varies, but often a minimum £25 up to maximum £10,000, plus reinvested certificates of up to £10,000 in value.

Watch out. Good in times of high inflation, but a poor rate of interest in times of low inflation or if you cash in early. And keep an eye on the general extension rate because it can be very low. (The general extension rate is the interest you get after the certificates have matured.)

> **Tip**
> If you have bought your full allowance of savings certificates and still want more, buy them in trust and you double your allowance.

Annuities

At this stage you could be thinking of buying an annuity. This is a life insurance policy in reverse. Instead of paying monthly premiums and getting a lump sum in the end, you pay in a lump sum and get monthly payments to the end!

The actuaries at the insurance companies use statistics to work out how long you are likely to live, take on board likely interest rates and make you an offer for your lump sum.

The older you are before you buy the annuity the more you get, so it is worth putting it off until you are over seventy-five.

Drawback

The problem with an annuity is that you don't know how long you are going to live. If you buy at age seventy-five and live to collect your telegram from the Queen you'll do well out of it. If you fall under a bus the day after you pay over your cash you'll do very badly.

You can guarantee the policy so that it pays out for a certain number of years even if you die in the meantime, or so that your estate will get part of your lump sum back if you die in the first few years, but of course that will cost money. You will have to forfeit part of the monthly payment. Most people take a five-year guarantee, though you can opt for a ten-year one. With a couple, there is no point in taking out this type of insurance as the policy runs to the second death.

- A man of eighty with a £20,000 lump sum would be likely to get a monthly payment of £250.
- A woman of eighty with the same money might get £220.
- You can also buy an annuity on a joint-life basis, so a man of eighty with a seventy-five-year-old wife paying in £20,000 might get £180. And that would be paid until the second partner dies.

TAKING A JOB

Work, after work, can take on many forms. You may need proper employment to keep body and soul together if your pension and savings are not adequate to maintain your lifestyle. You may want a part-time job just to supplement your income. Or you may prefer voluntary work for the social value.

But whatever it is you decide to do, for whatever reasons, if you are paid, it will affect three things:

- your pension
- your tax
- your benefits.

Pension

If you are already claiming your pension, then it won't be affected by any money you are paid from your job. Neither your state pension nor any company pension or private pension plan will be affected by your earnings.

However, if you decide to delay taking your pension because of your new work, what you get, eventually, will be affected. All types of pension will pay more to you when you claim, simply because you have delayed taking any money.

Your state pension, however, should not be postponed by more than five years because after that it won't be increased by any more, so you might as well claim it.

Tax

Any money you earn must be declared to the Inland Revenue so that you can be taxed on it. Earnings might take you into the tax system, or into a higher tax bracket.

If you are over sixty-five, extra income could push you over the age allowance limit – £14,200 in the 1993–4 tax year. That will have a dramatic influence on your tax position (see page 126 for full details). If your earnings are taking you marginally over the level, it might be worth working a few hours less in order to stay within the limits. Or juggle your savings so as to go for capital growth instead of income.

And if you are working and your spouse isn't, you may want to move the family savings into your partner's name. That way you'll get more interest on your money if your partner's a non-taxpayer and you pay tax, or your partner pays at a lower rate.

Benefits

If you are taking a job solely to increase your income because you don't have enough to live on, think twice before you start work.

Pensioners on benefit will lose out if their income rises. Income Support will be deducted on a pound-for-pound basis. So for every extra pound you earn, a pound will be deducted from your benefit.

Income Support is a 'passport' benefit – that means you get a lot of extras with it. You might get housing benefit, free NHS dental treatment, vouchers for glasses, wigs and fabric supports, and travel costs to and from hospitals. So an extra pound or two a week from a job may cost you a lot more than that in lost benefits.

Your local CAB or money advice centre would be able to do your sums for you to work out whether you'd be better with a job or with your benefits.

18 Making Ends Meet

How to raise money on your property · home income plans · annuities · mortgages · home reversion schemes

For most people their house is their most valuable asset; when they retire, they often take the opportunity of selling and moving into something smaller. This makes a lot of sense, as they can reduce their outgoings in line with the reduction in income and it will also release capital.

But the nineties have seen a new phenomenon for many people – falling house prices. This has meant either less money when the property is sold or, often, forcing the decision in favour of staying put.

But even with falling prices, many older people still have a valuable asset in bricks and mortar – but only on paper. The phrase 'house rich, cash poor' has been coined to fit their particular situation. However, it is possible to use a property as a means of increasing your income without going to all the trouble of selling up and moving down-market. There are two ways of doing this:

- By taking out a mortgage and putting the cash into an annuity – normally called a home income plan. The cash paid by the annuity pays off the interest owing on the mortgage, and the balance is paid over to you.
- By selling a 'share' of your property to a specialist company and using the cash to buy an annuity – often called a home reversion scheme.

HOME INCOME PLANS

This type of plan is also called a mortgage annuity plan, simply because it makes use of these two separate financial tools. In a nutshell, you take out a mortgage and buy an annuity which gives you an income for life.

We looked at annuities in Chapter 12 when the time came to arrange your pension and the principles here are exactly the same. The annuity is taken out with an insurance company and how much you get depends largely on your sex and age, and current interest rates.

You are guaranteed the income for life and when the surviving spouse dies, the income dies too.

To qualify for a home income plan you have to be:

- At least seventy, or have a combined age of 150 if you are a couple.
- The property has to be freehold or a long lease of more than perhaps fifty or sixty years.
- You do not have to be a married couple. For example two partners living together, two sisters or even brother and sister will normally qualify.

A home income plan works like this:

- You take out a mortgage on your property, normally up to a maximum of 80 per cent of its value.
- The cash you raise goes to buy an annuity which gives you an income for life, normally paid monthly.
- Generally the maximum loan will be for £30,000, because this is the limit for tax relief on the mortgage interest.
- You can usually take 10 per cent of the loan in cash – you may need to do urgent house repairs – but the rest has to go towards the annuity.
- The loan is interest-only and the capital is repaid when the house is sold, which will be when you or your surviving partner dies.
- Interest can either be fixed at the outset or vary when the

rates change. Most retired people prefer fixed rates so they know exactly where they are.

- The income you raise from the annuity first of all goes to pay the interest. What is left over is your spending money.
- Tax relief on home income plans remains at 25 per cent.

Example

If a man aged seventy obtained a loan of £30,000 and took cash of £3,000, the balance would provide a net monthly income, after mortgage interest and 25 per cent tax, of £955.80 a year or £79.65 a month.

Points to watch

- The annuity can be on your life only, or on both your lives if you have a partner. If you die shortly after signing up, the money will be wasted. To cover this, many plans have a 'capital protection' clause which says that only part of the loan will have to be repaid if you die in the first three or four years. This means that your heirs will get more money. However, in return for this protection, you will get lower monthly income.
- The additional income you get could push you into a tax-paying bracket. If this affects you, ask for a non-tax-basis scheme to avoid paying any extra to the taxman. If you are receiving any social security benefits, you should also make sure that these will not be affected by the extra money you will be getting.
- Most home-income-plan companies require the annuity and loan to be with them, so there is no choice. In other cases a proper scheme has to be established.

Pros

- The house remains yours at all times. This means that any increase in value is also yours.

- If you decide to sell the property and move elsewhere the loan can be repaid but the annuity will continue.
- As long as a new property is suitable, the loan can often be transferred to it.
- The mortgage can reduce your inheritance tax bill, as it will be deducted from your total assets.
- If you are a non-taxpayer, the income can be paid gross – that is, there will be no tax deduction.

Cons

- The amounts you can raise are generally limited and as most of the money goes towards an annuity, you cannot get your hands on a lot of ready cash.
- There will be extra charges to pay, such as survey and solicitor's fees.
- The annuity stops on death – or on the death of the surviving spouse.
- There will be less money to leave to your heirs.

HOME REVERSION SCHEMES

This type of scheme involves selling all or part of your house to the lender. In return you will, depending on the scheme, get either an annuity or a lump sum in cash, which is basically yours to do what you will with. However, most people buy an annuity to increase their income.

- You and your spouse have the right to live in the house for the rest of your lives.
- When you die – or your spouse if you die first – the property belongs to the reversion company.

If you give up the right to the whole of the property, you will have to pay a nominal 'peppercorn' rent, but this will be no more than a £1 a month or so. However, you will still be responsible for the upkeep and the running costs.

A reversion does have the advantage of raising more money

than an income plan and you will have more cash to spend. When you take out an annuity, you buy it with your own money and there is no interest to pay back. It also suits those people with few close relations or whose immediate family are already comfortably off. But there are some major drawbacks which you will have to offset against the increased cash.

Drawbacks

- The value placed on the house will be well below its true market value. In a period of falling house prices, it is in any case difficult to estimate what a house is actually worth. But you can generally guarantee that the price the reversion company places on it will be no more than around 50 per cent of its value.
- The younger you are, the less you will get.
- With most schemes, you lose out on any future increases in the value of your property, which will go to the reversion company. But at least one company will provide for annuity increases if house prices go up.
- You cannot leave your house to your heirs.
- It will not be easy to move house in the future.

Selling part of your property

Because of the potential drawbacks with the basic scheme, a few specialist companies have come up with a variety of other possibilities. These involve selling only part of the property, which means that you can leave the rest to your family. In addition, there are schemes which will allow you to share in future price rises and at the same time draw extra cash.

A recently introduced plan allows you to sell your house in slices of, say, 20 per cent. In return, you get a guaranteed income for the next five years. At the end of this period, you can sell another 20 per cent, and so on, until you reach the age of eighty-five, when the income is payable for life.

This scheme allows you to profit from a rising property market and, at the same time, leave something to your heirs.

Do consult with your immediate family and a solicitor before taking a decision, and make sure you get reliable and independent advice.

INVESTMENT BOND SCHEMES

If anyone suggests an investment bond scheme of any sort, politely withdraw from the conversation. These are normally far too risky for older people on restricted incomes. There is generally no guarantee that they will do well and, if they fail, you could end up with a lot less money and no home.

DO IT YOURSELF

There is nothing to stop you from arranging your own remortgage or taking out any form of loan against your property. There are plenty of mortgage companies which will lend to older people on an interest-only basis, with the basic loan being repaid when the property is sold.

But do be extremely wary of schemes which 'roll-over' the interest. It may sound attractive to have nothing to pay back. But the interest doesn't disappear. It is simply added to the outstanding amount, which will grow and grow, and there is no tax relief. If interest rates are high, the amount you owe can double every six or seven years and the loan will soon be more than the house is worth.

19 When Someone Dies

What to do about tax · benefits · pensions · debt · thinking ahead

See also: Chapter 9, Wills and Inheritance Tax Planning

Losing a loved one, at any age, is a traumatic experience. But it can be particularly difficult when you are older, simply because you have lived together for so long. On top of the emotional strain that you are under, there are a number of financial decisions that have to be taken. If it is at all possible, put these off for a few months.

Decisions taken in haste are invariably the wrong ones. Many's the person who has sold up after the death of a spouse and regretted it for ever after. So don't be rushed into doing anything that could wait for three months.

Financially, there will be three main areas which will change on the death of your partner.

- tax
- benefits
- pension.

TAX

When you are married, you both get a personal allowance and a married couple's allowance. Nowadays you can choose which partner the married couple's allowance will be paid to. If your partner dies early in the year, you should write to your tax inspector to make sure that any unused portion of the married couple's allowance is transferred to you. The personal allowance is not transferable. Age allowance is not transferable either, so if you are under sixty-five when your spouse dies, the age allowance will be lost. Your own tax threshold will be unchanged.

Widows, but not widowers, get an additional tax benefit known as the widow's bereavement allowance. This raises the tax-free threshold for them in the tax year following the one in which their husband dies. For the tax year 1993–4 the allowance is £1,720; it is usually increased each year in the Budget. If a widow or widower has children under the age of eighteen, they can claim an additional personal allowance – £1,720 for 1993–4. This allowance can only be claimed once, regardless of how many children there are.

BENEFITS

Traditionally, a husband is the wage-earner of the family so, both tax-wise and benefit-wise, widows do much better than widowers.

The DSS have three main benefits for widows, providing they are under sixty-five when their husband dies.

- Widow's Payment
- Widowed Mother's Allowance
- Widow's pension.

Widow's Payment

This is a lump-sum payment of £1,000 and is paid regardless of how rich or poor you are. It is dependent on your late husband's National Insurance contributions. You must be under sixty to claim, or under sixty-five if your husband was not getting a state pension. If you're not sure whether you qualify, claim anyway. It is paid once as a lump sum and is tax-free.

Widowed Mother's Allowance

If you have children and are getting child benefit you will qualify for this allowance. It is paid in two parts – a portion for you and a portion for your children. So what you get depends on how many children you have. It is paid weekly and is taxable.

Widow's pension

You qualify for this if you are over forty-five when your husband dies or when your widowed mother's allowance ends. It is a weekly payment, and you get more when you are fifty-four, but it will be stopped if you remarry or move in with another man. It is paid weekly until you are sixty and qualify for a state retirement pension, and it is taxable; if you are not eligible for the full state pension, any shortfall should be made up by Income Support.

Other DSS help

Both widows and widowers can claim other benefits from the DSS. If you have too little coming in, it is worth applying for Income Support, Housing Benefit, Family Credit if you have children, and Council-tax Benefit. Your local DSS office should be able to help you to work out whether or not you qualify, or ring a DSS freephone helpline – 0800 666555. Alternatively, go along to your local Citizens Advice Bureau and ask them to help you with your finances.

Tip
Remember, if you qualify for Income Support you will get other financial help automatically, such as free prescriptions and dental treatment. So even if you only get a pound or two a week, it is worth claiming in order to get the add-ons.

PENSIONS

State

When your partner dies, the state pension will die with them. You can keep the pension for the week in which the person dies, but you can't claim for the next week. A wife on a dependant's pension of £33.70 would have her money raised to a single person's pension of £56.10.

Company

If the husband dies, the wife will still get part of his pension paid to her by the company. How much she gets will depend on the terms of the scheme but it could be more than you think, because you get a percentage, say half, of the original pension – not the amount you were receiving after any lump sum was taken out. Usually widowers get similar treatment. Most pensions are guaranteed for five years, so if you die within that period your spouse should get a lump-sum equivalent to what you have not been paid. See Chapter 3.

Personal

It depends on which option you took when you retired. If you made allowances for your partner, they will get a pension. If not, they won't.

COUNCIL TAX

If you are living alone in your house after your partner dies you can claim a 25 per cent reduction on the council tax.

DEBT

One of the few things you do take on to the next world are your debts. If you die penniless, your debts will be written off. But if there is money in the estate from insurance policies, pensions, savings accounts or the house then these will have to be used to pay the debts. However, a widow should never use her money – such as the widow's payment – to clear her late husband's debts.

Tip
Check any loans that you have taken out in case you are paying for life insurance. This could mean that the loan is paid off when your husband (wife) dies. Some of these you actually have to opt out of, rather than opt in, so you might have this insurance without knowing it.

THINKING AHEAD

The death of a partner is an emotionally draining experience for all the family left behind. Dealing with death is never easy, but it can be made much more difficult if you have to cope with muddled money problems as well.

So this can be a good time to make sure that you will not be leaving a similar situation when you go.

It is worth spending a bit of time now, to ensure that everything will be in good order when your time comes. Start by checking out Chapter 9, Wills and Inheritance Tax Planning, to ensure that you are doing everything possible to reduce your inheritance tax bill.

On top of the suggestions there, other more financially sophisticated moves can be made. Loan trusts, for example, allow you to have your cake and eat it. You can set up a trust for your children, loan it a lump sum interest-free, but reclaim 5 per cent of the capital yourself each year. The money in the trust, however, doesn't go down by 5 per cent a year because investment return will keep it growing.

But trusts like this must be set up by a professional – so take advice from a financial adviser who is used to setting up these trusts.

20 Independent Financial Advice

Where to go to get help if you have financial problems · how to complain if you feel you have been badly treated

Financial Services Act

This Act came into force in 1988 in stages and covers all investments – unit trusts, life insurance policies, shares, etc., but not things like bank or building society accounts, as these are not, strictly speaking, investments.

The Act established the Securities and Investments Board, which oversees all investment business carried out in this country. Known as SIB, it has in turn set up four separate watchdogs which regulate sections of the investment industry. These are called self-regulatory organizations (SROs) and are:

- FIMBRA (Financial Intermediaries, Managers and Brokers Regulatory Association) covers many of the insurance brokers and financial advisers giving independent financial advice.
- IMRO (Investment Managers Regulatory Organization) – the members include unit trust, insurance, investment trust and pension-fund managements.
- LAUTRO (Life Assurance and Unit Trust Regulatory Organization), which covers insurance companies, friendly societies and unit trust companies.
- SFA (Securities and Futures Association), which covers stockbrokers and securities dealers and dealers in the futures and options markets.

Anyone carrying on investment business in Britain must be authorized by one of the above four watchdogs, or directly by SIB. However, members of professional bodies – solicitors and accountants, for example, who only do a limited amount of investment business, can get authorization direct from their association, the Law Society or the Institute of Chartered Accountants. This also applies to general insurance brokers doing some investment business, who can be regulated by the Insurance Brokers' Registration Council.

Before authorization is given, the person applying is checked out carefully to make sure they have a clean record and adequate financial resources. It is a criminal offence to carry on investment business unless you are authorized.

It is therefore vital that investors check that they are dealing with an authorized adviser – letterheads and business cards must state clearly the organization which has given authorization. You can ring SIB (see Appendix 2) to check that you are talking to an authorized firm. (Make sure you have the full name before checking.)

The difference between independent advisers and tied agents

Not all advisers are alike. Some will be independent, others will work for just one company. Potential investors should realize that the difference between the two can have a great deal of bearing on their choice of investment:

- Independent advisers work for themselves and for their clients. They have to give you the best available advice, and this means looking at the whole range of products on the market, not just a limited number. They must give you a FIMBRA Buyer's Guide which makes their status clear and sets out your rights.
- Tied agents are just that – tied to one company only. They will only sell the products of that specific company and, by definition, have a vested interest in promoting its policies. They must give you a LAUTRO Buyer's Guide which shows their tied status and explains your rights.

An adviser should make it very clear at the outset whether he or she is independent or tied. If you are unsure, ask.

HOW TO COMPLAIN

If you have a complaint against an adviser, your first step should be to take the matter up with him. If that does not bring results, then write to the chief executive of the organization that he works for.

If that still does not resolve the problem, your next step is to get in touch with the organization which has authorized him.

Every SRO has set up a complaints procedure to help investors with a problem. Ring the watchdog (see Appendix 2) and explain what your problem is. They will probably tell you which steps to take next. If the SRO cannot help, it will tell you where you can take your complaint next.

Also, every SRO has appointed an ombudsman or referee to investigate investors' problems on a completely impartial basis. All have the power to make substantial financial awards if they decide the adviser has been negligent.

Warning

These SROs and ombudsmen cannot help you with disappointing investment performance. So if your investment has dropped in value by half through normal market forces, there is nothing they can do. What they will look at is cases where the wrong type of investment has been recommended, or where money has been fraudulently misused.

The ombudsmen

- Banking Ombudsman
- Insurance Ombudsman
- Investment Referee
- Building Society Ombudsman
- Pensions Ombudsman/OPAS
- Ombudsman of Corporate Estate Agents.

The Investment Referee and Insurance Ombudsman can award compensation of up to £100,000 when they investigate cases and find the company is responsible for the problem. But the FIMBRA arbitration scheme is limited to a maximum of £50,000 compensation.

Plans are now being discussed to bring all the retail regulatory organizations under one roof – under a new body to be set up called the Personal Investment Authority (PIA). One of its main attractions for investors is that there would be just one central point to which all complaints could be made.

COMPENSATION

There are a number of compensation funds in place which will pay out cash if an adviser or company goes bust.

The SIB compensation fund (the Investment Compensation Scheme)

This pays out compensation of 100 per cent of the first £30,000 invested, then 90 per cent of the next £20,000 – making a total maximum of £48,000. This compensation scheme covers all four watchdogs and can pay out a maximum of £100 million a year.

Banks and deposit-takers

This covers all banks and deposit-takers classified by the Bank of England as 'authorized institutions'. It pays out compensation equal to 75 per cent of the first £20,000 invested – a maximum of £15,000.

Building society compensation fund

This covers all members of the Corporation of Mortgage Lenders – building societies and other mortgage lenders. It pays out compensation equal to 90 per cent of the first £20,000 invested – a maximum of £18,000.

Policyholders Protection Act

This covers all authorized British life insurance companies and provides 90 per cent of the benefits promised by the insurance company in the unlikely event that it should go bust – provided the benefits promised were not excessive.

PENSIONS PROBLEMS

If you have a problem with your company pension scheme or a personal pension plan which you can't resolve with your employer, or the company running the scheme, you can get help and advice from the Occupational Pensions Advisory Service (OPAS). You can contact them through your local Citizens Advice Bureau (or see Appendix 2).

OPAS is an independent voluntary organization with a network of 250 advisers throughout the country. But if OPAS cannot help then you can take your complaint to the Pensions Ombudsman, who is empowered to investigate complaints about injustice caused by the maladministration of the trustees or managers of a company or personal pension scheme, and disputes of fact or law with the trustees or managers.

However neither OPAS nor the Pensions Ombudsman can help on problems over state pensions.

PROBLEMS WITH STOCKBROKERS

The Stock Exchange and the Securities and Futures Association have set up a Complaints Bureau which is run by an independent commissioner. You should first of all try to resolve the problem by writing to the chief executive at the company for whom the stockbroker works. But if that does not resolve the matter, then you can contact the Complaints Bureau at the Securities and Futures Association (see Appendix 2).

If you are still not satisfied, you can go to one of the bureau's two arbitration schemes. One is the consumer arbitration scheme, which for a £10 fee investigates disputes involving sums up to £25,000. There is also an arbitration scheme which handles disputes over larger sums of money and is likely to be more expensive.

APPENDIX 1

Questions to Ask

QUESTIONS TO ASK YOURSELF

- Are you a financial risk taker or a safety-first player?
- Would you rather have a steady income, or are you prepared to accept the peaks and troughs that come through investing in shares?
- Do you like and trust the financial adviser you are dealing with? You are likely to be in regular contact so it is important to feel happy about the relationship.
- Are the returns paid by the investment significantly higher than those paid by other investments of a similar nature? If they are – be cautious.
- Does the adviser want to spend some time with you talking over your financial position, family commitments, lifestyle plans, etc.? If an adviser seems rushed, and does not ask you many questions, there is a good chance he or she is only interested in your money.
- Has your adviser been in business for some time – always a good sign – and what are his offices like? Very luxurious offices and flash cars are no guarantee of quality advice.

QUESTIONS TO ASK YOUR FINANCIAL ADVISER

- Are you an independent financial adviser or do you only sell the products of one company?
- By which self-regulatory organization are you authorized? What is the full name and address of your company so I can check it out with the SRO?

- How much commission will you earn by selling me the policy? How does this vary from the commission to be earned on other policies you have recommended?
- What are the policy charges and are they likely to escalate?

QUESTIONS TO ASK ON LEAVING A JOB WITH A COMPANY PENSION SCHEME

- Ask what transfer value the company is prepared to pay if you take your pension rights away from the company scheme.
- Ask the adviser whether you are better off taking your pension rights with you to a new employer, leaving them with your existing employer or transferring them to an insurance plan.
- Ask the adviser whether he uses one of the analysis services to evaluate whether you would do better leaving your pension rights where they are or switching them.
- If the adviser recommends switching the pension rights to a personal personal pension plan or Section 32 buy-out bond, ask for clear reasons why he thinks this is the best course available.
- Ask him how much commission he will earn by switching your cash into an insurance product and whether he is prepared to split it and pay half the commission back into the policy to enhance your retirement nest-egg.
- When buying personal pensions remember there are around a hundred different companies running plans. Why has the adviser suggested a particular company? Has he got performance tables to show how well they have done in the past? (But remember past performance is no guarantee of future performance.)
- When your adviser recommends switching from one plan to another, make sure there are good reasons for the switch, as you will incur heavy charges every time you move your money from one company to another.

QUESTIONS TO ASK WHEN INVESTING THE PROCEEDS OF YOUR PERSONAL PENSION PLAN TO PROVIDE YOU WITH AN INCOME FOR LIFE

- Are you suggesting I buy the annuity from the same company I saved up with?

- Have you checked around to find out if other companies are offering better returns than the company with which I saved?
- Should I opt for an annuity which pays a level pension, or one that starts off a bit lower, but goes up every year, either by a set amount or in line with the retail prices index?
- What level of pension can I expect if I arrange it so that my wife gets half the pension if I die first?

QUESTIONS TO ASK YOUR EMPLOYER

- What happens to my pension rights if I become ill, or die, before retirement age?
- What are the arrangements if I want to retire early? By how much will my pension be reduced?
- What are the rules/options about the female retirement age – and if the age has been equalized with men, is the new policy being phased in or introduced immediately?
- By how much have pensions in payment been increased recently?
- What pension will my spouse get if I die first?

APPENDIX 2
Useful Addresses

Association of British Insurers
51 Gresham Street
London EC2V 7HQ
071–600 3333

Association of Investment Trust Companies
Park House
16 Finsbury Circus
London EC2M 7JJ
071–588 5347

Association of Policy Marketmakers
4 Sullbridge Mill
Maldon
Essex CM9 7FN
0621 851133

Banking Information Service
10 Lombard Street
London EC3V 9AP
071–626 8486

Banking Ombudsman
Citadel House
5–11 Fetter Lane
London EC4A 1BR
071–583 1395

British Insurance and Investment Brokers Association (BIIBA)
BIIBA House
14 Bevis Marks
London EC3A 7NT
071–623 9043

Building Societies Association (Council of Mortgage Lenders)
3 Saville Row
London WIX IAF
071–437 0655

Building Societies Ombudsman
35–7 Grosvenor Gardens
London SWIX 7AW
071–931 0044

Consumers' Association
2 Marylebone Road
London NWI 4DF
071–486 5544

Department for National Savings
Charles House
375 Kensington High Street
London WI4 8SD
071–605 9300

Estate Agents' Ombudsman
Suite 3, Old Library Chambers
Chipper Lane
Salisbury
Wilts SPI IYQ
0722 333306

Financial Intermediaries, Managers and Brokers
    Regulatory Association (FIMBRA)
Hertsmere House
Hertsmere Road
London EI4 4AB
071–538 8860

Freeline Social Security
(Gives free advice on Social Security benefits, pensions,
National Insurance, etc.)
0800 666555

A Guide to Grants for Individuals in Need
Available from:
Raduis Works
Back Lane
London NW3 1HL

Independent Financial Advice (IFA) Helpline
(will provide names and addresses of independent financial advisers
in your area)
0483 461461

Inland Revenue (see phone book for local office)
Somerset House
Strand
London WC2R 1LB
071–438 6622

Institute of Chartered Accountants
   (England and Wales)
Chartered Accountants Hall
Moorgate Place
London EC2P 2BJ
071–920 8100

Institute of Chartered Accountants (Scotland)
27 Queen Street
Edinburgh EH2 1LA
031–225 5673

Insurance Brokers Registration Council
15 St Helens Place
London EC3A 6DS
071–588 4387

Insurance Ombudsman (now includes unit trust ombudsman)
City Gate One
135 Park Street
London SE1 9EA
071–928 4488

Investment Managers' Regulatory Organization (IMRO)
Broadwalk House
5 Appold Street
London EC2A 2LL
071–628 6022

Law Society
113 Chancery Lane
London WC2A IPL
071–242 1222

Law Society (Scotland)
26 Drumsheugh Gardens
Edinburgh EH3 7YR

Life Assurance and Unit Trust Regulatory Organization
  (LAUTRO)
Centre Point
103 New Oxford Street
London WCIA IQH
071–379 0444

Occupational Pensions Advisory Service (OPAS)
11 Belgrave Road
London SWIV IRB
071–233 8080

Office of Fair Trading
Field House
Breams Building
London EC4A IPR
071–242 2858

Pensions Ombudsman
11 Belgrave Road
London SWIV IRB
071–834 9144

RPFA Unit (Retirement Pension Forecast Assessment)
Room 37d
Central Office
Newcastle upon Tyne NE98 IYX

Registrar of Friendly Societies
15 Great Marlborough Street
London WIV IAX
071–437 9992

The Securities and Futures Association (SFA)
Cotton Centre
Cotton Lane
London SEI 2QB
071–378 9000

Securities and Investments Board
Gavrelle House
2–14 Bunhill Row
London ECIY 8RA
071–638 1240

The Stock Exchange
Old Broad Street
London EC2N IHP
071–588 2355

Unit Trust Association
65 Kingsway
London WC2B 6TD
071–831 0898

Index

READ MORE IN PENGUIN

In every corner of the world, on every subject under the sun, Penguin represents quality and variety – the very best in publishing today.

For complete information about books available from Penguin – including Puffins, Penguin Classics and Arkana – and how to order them, write to us at the appropriate address below. Please note that for copyright reasons the selection of books varies from country to country.

In the United Kingdom: Please write to *Dept. JC, Penguin Books Ltd, FREEPOST, West Drayton, Middlesex UB7 OBR*

If you have any difficulty in obtaining a title, please send your order with the correct money, plus ten per cent for postage and packaging, to *PO Box No. 11, West Drayton, Middlesex UB7 OBR*

In the United States: Please write to *Penguin USA Inc., 375 Hudson Street, New York, NY 10014*

In Canada: Please write to *Penguin Books Canada Ltd, 10 Alcorn Avenue, Suite 300, Toronto, Ontario M4V 3B2*

In Australia: Please write to *Penguin Books Australia Ltd, 487 Maroondah Highway, Ringwood, Victoria 3134*

In New Zealand: Please write to *Penguin Books (NZ) Ltd,182–190 Wairau Road, Private Bag, Takapuna, Auckland 9*

In India: Please write to *Penguin Books India Pvt Ltd, 706 Eros Apartments, 56 Nehru Place, New Delhi 110 019*

In the Netherlands: Please write to *Penguin Books Netherlands B.V., Keizersgracht 231 NL–1016 DV Amsterdam*

In Germany: Please write to *Penguin Books Deutschland GmbH, Friedrichstrasse 10–12, W–6000 Frankfurt/Main 1*

In Spain: Please write to *Penguin Books S. A., C. San Bernardo 117–6° E–28015 Madrid*

In Italy: Please write to *Penguin Italia s.r.l., Via Felice Casati 20, I–20124 Milano*

In France: Please write to *Penguin France S. A., 17 rue Lejeune, F–31000 Toulouse*

In Japan: Please write to *Penguin Books Japan, Ishikiribashi Building, 2–5–4, Suido, Tokyo 112*

In Greece: Please write to *Penguin Hellas Ltd, Dimocritou 3, GR–106 71 Athens*

In South Africa: Please write to *Longman Penguin Southern Africa (Pty) Ltd, Private Bag X08, Bertsham 2013*

READ MORE IN PENGUIN

A CHOICE OF NON-FICTION

Riding the Iron Rooster Paul Theroux

Travels in old and new China with the author of *The Great Railway Bazaar*. 'Mr Theroux cannot write badly ... he is endlessly curious about places and people ... and in the course of a year there was almost no train in the whole vast Chinese rail network in which he did not travel' – Ludovic Kennedy

Ninety-two Days Evelyn Waugh

In this fascinating chronicle of a South American journey, Waugh describes the isolated cattle country of Guiana, sparsely populated by an odd collection of visionaries, rogues and ranchers, and records the nightmarish experiences travelling on foot, by horse and by boat through the jungle in Brazil.

The Life of Graham Greene Norman Sherry
Volume One 1904–1939

'Probably the best biography ever of a living author' – Philip French in the *Listener*. Graham Greene has always maintained a discreet distance from his reading public. This volume reconstructs his first thirty-five years to create one of the most revealing literary biographies of the decade.

The Day Gone By Richard Adams

In this enchanting memoir the bestselling author of *Watership Down* tells his life story from his idyllic 1920s childhood spent in Newbury, Berkshire, through public school, Oxford and service in World War Two to his return home and his courtship of the girl he was to marry.

A Turn in the South V. S. Naipaul

'A supremely interesting, even poetic glimpse of a part of America foreigners either neglect or patronize' – *Guardian*. 'An extraordinary panorama' – *Daily Telegraph*. 'A fine book by a fine man, and one to be read with great enjoyment: a book of style, sagacity and wit' – *Sunday Times*

READ MORE IN PENGUIN

A CHOICE OF NON-FICTION

1001 Ways to Save the Planet   Bernadette Vallely

There are 1001 changes that *everyone* can make in their lives today to bring about a greener environment – whether at home or at work, on holiday or away on business. Action that you can take *now*, and that you won't find too difficult to take. This practical guide shows you how.

Bitter Fame   Anne Stevenson

'A sobering and salutary attempt to estimate what Plath was, what she achieved and what it cost her ... This is the only portrait which answers Ted Hughes's image of the poet as Ariel, not the ethereal bright pure roving sprite, but Ariel trapped in Prospero's pine and raging to be free' – *Sunday Telegraph*

The Complete Book of Running   James F. Fixx

Jim Fixx's pioneering book has encouraged a sedentary generation to take to the streets. Packed with information for the beginner, the more experienced runner and the marathon winner, it explains the many benefits to be reaped from running and advises on how to overcome the difficulties. 'This book is a boon and a blessing to the multitudes who jog and run throughout the world' – Michael Parkinson

Friends in High Places   Jeremy Paxman

'The Establishment is alive and well ... in pursuit of this elusive, seminal circle of souls around which British institutions revolve, Jeremy Paxman ... has written a thoughtful examination, both poignant and amusing' – *Independent*

Slow Boats to China   Gavin Young

Gavin Young's bestselling account of his extraordinary journey in small boats through the Mediterranean, the Red Sea, the Indian Ocean and the Malaya and China Seas to China. 'A joy to read, engaging, civilised, sharply observant, richly descriptive and sometimes hilarious ... a genuine modern adventure story' – *Sunday Express*

READ MORE IN PENGUIN

A CHOICE OF NON-FICTION

When Shrimps Learn to Whistle Denis Healey

Taking up the most powerful political themes that emerged from his hugely successful *The Time of My Life*, Denis Healey now gives us this stimulating companion volume. 'Forty-three years of ruminations ... by the greatest foreign secretary (as the author quietly and reasonably implies) we never had' – Ben Pimlott in the *New Statesman & Society*

Eastern Approaches Fitzroy Maclean

'The author's record of personal achievement is remarkable. The canvas which he covers is immense. The graphic writing reveals the ruthless man of action ... He emerges from [his book] as an extrovert Lawrence' – *The Times Literary Supplement*

This Time Next Week Leslie Thomas

'Mr Thomas's book is all humanity, to which is added a Welshman's mastery of words ... Some of his episodes are hilarious, some unbearably touching, but everyone, staff and children, is looked upon with compassion' – *Observer*. 'Admirably written, with clarity, realism, poignancy and humour' – *Daily Telegraph*

Reports from the Holocaust Larry Kramer

'A powerful book ... more than a political autobiography, *Reports* is an indictment of a world that allows AIDS to continue ... he is eloquent and convincing when he swings from the general to the specific. His recommendations on the release of drugs to AIDS patients are practical and humane' – *New York Newsday*

City on the Rocks Kevin Rafferty

'Rafferty has filled a glaring gap on the Asian bookshelf, offering the only comprehensive picture of Hong Kong right up to the impact of the Tiananmen Square massacre' – *Business Week*. 'A story of astonishing achievement, but its purpose is warning rather than celebration' – *Sunday Times*